Mojave Mysteries

(Volume One)

M.L. Behrman

PUBLISHED BY:
VM LLC
ISBN-10:1540583864
ISBN-13:978-1540583864
Copyright © 2016 M.L. Behrman
All rights reserved.

Table of Contents

"I am a great admirer of mystery and magic. Look at this life - all mystery and magic."

-Harry Houdini

The Mojave Desert

Located in the southwest of the United States, the Mojave Desert is many things; vast, seemingly empty, beautifully fragile and harshly unforgiving. Over the ages it has been home to countless tribes of tough indigenous peoples, as well as travelers, self-styled prophets and complete madmen drawn to the undeniable feeling of natural power and inherent spirituality it so readily projects. Miners and fortune seekers have also covered it from one end to the other in the forlorn hopes of forcing the great Mojave to yield its immense deposits of mineral riches. I love it and have been a fan of the open spaces and rocky precipices for years, hiking and camping as much as time allows. Sitting under the blazing stars around a small camp fire out in the desert after a day of exploring is a simple pleasure to which few things can compare.

But this isn't a guide book full of innocuous tales of benign family fun and lazy adventures, because I also love a good mystery - the more bizarre, monstrous and unexplainable the better! And the desert thankfully offers these strange stories in spades, made all the crazier and chilling by the remoteness and other-worldly aspects of the location. This book is a small collection of some of the more interesting and extraordinary tales I have come across or heard about over the years, sometimes from the participants themselves or their descendants. Many have wanted their names left unrecorded, but where applicable I have used public records or news accounts to validate the story. As to the veracity of their tales, I leave it to the reader, as at the end of the day any good mystery is just that – something that just can't be explained or understood within a conventional framework. I don't claim this to be an exhaustive encyclopedia of events either, merely my rather eclectic collection of crazy stuff I have come across in my explorations and research. My only criteria for inclusion is this; did it leave me shaking my head and going *whoa!*

Let's get started!

Devils, Cults and Demon Flyers

If you're looking for a remote spot to hone your vision and meditate upon the divine nature of the cosmos, the desert is the spot. A long line of prophets and religious leaders over the centuries have proved that. Nothing beats sitting on a high rocky outcrop or open space and watching the sun go down while pondering the meaning of life or simply enjoying the beauty of nature and creation. But, the desert also has that same draw for another type of personality; those that want to use its remoteness as cover for their crimes and warped cult activities. Whether it's the wacky drugged-out ravings and murders of someone like Charles Manson and his "family" or the numerous black mass and "demonic" societies that often practice their evil far into the interior, the desert has given birth – and more often death, to many inclined to the dark side. I have more than a few cases of the strange and bizarre relating to this malevolent aspect of the beautiful Mojave's spiritual consciousness in my files, but first want to relate something that happened to me personally.

It's no surprise that as I love to wander and explore out in the desert I've come across more than a few things that have left me scratching my head. But few have made me feel there was a genuine evil or darkness to their existence more than the following little story.

I often just travel about in my jeep visiting the long abandoned or ruined cabins that dot the desert in untold numbers, taking pictures and poking about to discover just what people were doing out there in the middle of seemingly nowhere. Often the ruined shack or cabin is testimony to the failed dreams of a mining operation or desperate homesteading, other times you just know there was something going on that would take someone with the observational and deductive skills of Sherlock Holmes to unravel. Back in 2006 I was motoring along an old dirt track out in the Mojave south of Barstow near Ord Mountain just kind of drifting and "seeing what I could see" when I spotted an old wrecked cabin out on a flat spot near a ravine. As there were no signs or warnings that it was private property, and the trail to it didn't look as it had been recently traveled, I cruised over and parked. It was your fairly common 1930's style cabin with a couple of rooms, iron stove in the corner and an outhouse just near the back door. The tar paper roof had mostly collapsed and the plasterboard walls were pretty much broken out and shot full of holes – unfortunately a natural fate of anything left unattended in the desert. It sat on a concrete slab so I didn't have to worry about snakes under the rotten floorboards, I just had to keep an eye out for the numerous rusty nails that poked up from the collapsed roof beams (cheap 2x4's actually) and make sure I didn't impale myself on anything nasty. The first and main room was empty other than a moldy ripped up mattress in the corner and some broken beer bottles with scatterings of rat droppings. But it was in the second, more complete room that I came across something really shocking and also depressing.

Someone had painted a huge red dripping pentagram on the back wall, in the middle of which was nailed the crucified body of a large black desert raven. The body was desiccated and dried, but the huge wings were outspread and the beaked head still sat atop the slumped shoulders with its long sharp beak open in a silent scream. All around it was spray-painted numerous foul obscenities and bloody curses, directed mainly at women, and the repeated lines "this is for the master" and "I am coming for you" adorned the walls. Yikes! The whole thing just had the feeling of murderous insanity and mental sickness, obviously from the hand of some warped adult more than the misguided lark of drunk or goofy teenagers and I just spent a few more moments in the room before leaving without even taking a picture. Why record it? Who would want to look at that crap again? I have to admit I had to stifle the urge to just drop a match on the place and burn it down, but refrained. Stepping out the smashed doorway, I immediately looked around the ground to see if I could see any prints or signs that the person or persons who had done this might have recently visited, but saw nothing but my own boot prints and the tracks of a few animals. You can bet I also pulled out the binoculars and scanned the nearby hillsides to make sure nobody was even then watching me or their ghastly "shrine". I walked back to the jeep and left. The devil nonsense didn't really bother me as I think most that crap is a joke, but the misogynist threats and killing of an innocent animal bothered me and rather put a damper on the rest of my day trip. I had to wonder if the person that did that was capable of something even worse, and could only hope he had been locked up (or better yet, run over by a truck) before committing any further outrage. But as the following accounts will show, there seems to be a more than a few more others out there up to the same sort of mischief – or worse!

One rather horrid modern account I have is from a man, an "undocumented worker" as you will, who was hitchhiking from the aptly named Sandy Valley just along the California-Nevada state line down to Baker. He had been working as a house painter and had a friend in the small desert town who could hook him up with a crew that was doing private contracting jobs. Taking one of sole roads out of Sandy Valley, the man, whom we'll call "Antonio", was not having much luck, as the road is not that well-traveled and he had been hiking most of the day in a searing June heat. Arriving at the dirt turn-off into the Mesquite

Wilderness Area, he was sitting by the road finishing the rest of his water figuring he was going to have to spend the night laying on the hot ground just off the road when to his delight an old pickup came down the road and seeing him with his thumb out, actually stopped. Most people won't pick up hitchhikers in the best of areas, and finding someone way out in the desert either means they're lost, or worse, some whacko looking for trouble. But Antonio lucked out. And the better part of the deal was that the driver was an older woman in her fifties along with someone he took to be her daughter, a younger woman in her twenties. Anyone who's ever hitchhiked knows that it's a two-edged sword; you never know who's going to stop and sometimes they can be the nut! How many times have we heard of serial killers cruising the interstate just to find random and vulnerable victims? But the two women seemed friendly enough, so sliding in beside the daughter Antonio thanked them and although they said they were only going part way down to Baker, he was more than glad to get out of the burning desert sun. He had noticed they had some grocery bags in the back of the pickup and figured they were on their way back from the store.

As they motored along they didn't speak much, as Antonio's English isn't the best, but his pleasant demeanor and smile seemed to put the women at ease and the driver suggested that if he didn't mind detouring to their ranch for a short bit so they could get the groceries out of the sun, they would feed him and then take him at least down to the highway (Interstate I-15) so he could then continue on his way. He readily agreed.

Coming to an old road that branched off to the west, opposite the wilderness area, they drove along for about a half hour until they came to a rough trail that moved into a small canyon at the foot of some rocky hills. It wasn't much of a "ranch", more like a long trailer with the usual assortment of rusty metal and junked vehicles scattered around it that so many desert dwellers seem to inhabit. But free food was on the table and as Antonio said "much better than sleeping with the scorpions". After helping the two women with the bags of groceries, he waited outside as the forlorn trailer was cramped and "very messy. Not good house-keepers." He said that both women were very heavily tattooed and he thought the daughter might have been somewhat "retardado" as she never spoke and seemed to just obey the older woman's commands in silence with eyes downcast.

After a bit, the older woman came out with a plate of beans, hot dogs and a glass of lemonade, which being ice-cold, Antonio drained pretty much without waiting. He said that last thing he remembered was just tasting the beans when he pitched forward and it was lights out. Whatever they had dosed him with, he was certain it had been in the cold lemonade.

Coming to, the first thing he could make sense of was that he was tied up and laying on his side, with either a bag or blindfold over his eyes as he couldn't see a thing and had trouble breathing through the thick fabric. He was aware of voices around him, both male and female, as well as the sound of vehicles arriving and the loud crunching on the rocky ground as they stopped and the occupants got out. It seemed that people were assembling for something and at times would stand over him as if deciding what to do with him. Certain they were going to "break my head", he tried curling into a fetal position but a rough kick or poke would make him lie still and poor Antonio confessed he about wet himself from fear. And when he heard the bleating of a goat, a sound he was well familiar with from his youth in rural Mexico, his heart skipped a few beats as he was also aware of a sacrificial animal's role in the bloody rituals of the "Black Mass" practiced by more than a few narco-gangs or cartels down there. Was he going to be the human element to such a ceremony? His entrails used to adorn some shrine in a bloody offering to their dark lord? Hooded and trussed, he waited.

Soon his worst fears were realized as he heard the group assemble and start chanting, their voices rising and falling in a mumbling liturgy as a single male voice, deep and resonant, led them in ritual. All of a sudden Antonio felt two strong set of arms jerk him to his feet and half-drag him along for a short distance before depositing him on the ground where his hood or blindfold was pulled off and he could finally see the weird group assembled about him. In an instant, his blinking gaze was filled with the sight of a bunch of naked people, of pretty much all ages and sexes, smeared in blood and holding torches standing around him. On the ground, beside him sat the severed head of the goat, dropped into the center of a pentagram marked out on the desert gravel in small rocks and white chalk powder. The animal's intestines and internal organs were scattered about and in the hand of the man closest to him, one who the terrified laborer identified as the leader of group was the dripping heart of the butchered beast. "He was terrible to look at," Antonio recounted, "much tattooed and with silver pins in his face (*piercings?*). His eyes were mad."

The frightened hitchhiker was made to watch as the group now formed a line under the guidance of the "leader" and upon his command turned to the nearest person and began to have sex with them as the man with the "silver pins in his face" waved the heart about and chanted loudly. Antonio was especially shocked to see the older tattooed woman who had picked him up, having relations with the younger girl he had assumed was her daughter. And although

12

the blood-drenched activities would have been disquieting enough for most people, or maybe even titillating depending on one's proclivities, the idea that he might be next to go under the knife was the uppermost thought in the laborer's mind at the moment. Finally, after about ten minutes or so of the carnal escapades, the leader called a halt to the activities and the group turned their attention to the cowering Mexican hitchhiker on the ground. On command, two of the stronger members of the bloody covenant raced over to Antonio, and pinning him down held him tight as the leader came over and smeared him in a non-too gentle manner with the blood from the dripping goat heart by mashing it in his face.

Then casting the heart aside, the man took up a large knife that had been stuck in a nearby piece of firewood and waving it over his head while chanting, stood over Antonio and pointed it at the sky and then the terrified man's face three times in sequence. The group hushed. Poor Antonio was sure his moment had come.

Now here's where a strange story gets even stranger.

Suddenly, the young woman who the laborer had taken to be the somewhat "slow" daughter of his host threw herself on the ground with a scream and started thrashing about while starting to foam at the mouth as if having a seizure of some kind. Apparently, it was enough of a surprise to the others that their attention was momentarily diverted to the howling and writhing girl as her "mother" ran over and started trying to calm her accompanied by one or two others of the sect. Realizing this was probably his only chance, Antonio gave one of his distracted captors a mighty kick in the side with a free leg and before anyone could halt him, leapt to his feet and started out into the surrounding desert as fast as he could. The men holding him attempted to follow as the leader screamed at them, but as they were

naked and without shoes and Antonio was still wearing his
heavy work boots, he soon out-distanced them in the
darkness. Another thing that saved him as he related his
story later, was that they had tied his hands "like this, not like
this" as he demonstrated that his would-be jailers had trussed
his hands in front of his body rather than behind his back.
This allowed him to pretty much keep his balance and right
himself quickly enough when he did stumble and fall
occasionally while running across the uneven ground as fast
as his legs would carry him. After going some distance in a
blind panic, Antonio was relieved to find that his pursuers
had either given up or lost him in the darkness and he soon
found that the fire of the little enclave near the trailer was
but a flickering light some distance away.

Morning found the terrified hitchhiker making his way
across the desert and toward the direction where he thought
the dirt road had brought him into the area. He had gotten
his hands free by scraping the ropes binding them on a sharp
rock edge for "almost an hour" and was pretty sure he was
headed in the right direction. Finding the road, he followed it
back to the larger powerline road but always was careful not
to step on it lest he or his tracks be seen by any of the bloody
cultists if they were out driving the road still looking for him.
By late afternoon he had reached the main road, and
although racked by thirst and burnt by the Mojave sun, he
started down it hoping to eventually get to the highway and
thumb a ride or at least flag down a vehicle. "I cleaned my
face good with spit," he said, "the blood was dried but
smelled bad." Luckily for him, he never saw any trace of his
pursuers, and although he had to spend another night
crouched in some sheltering creosote bushes near the road,
by the next day he made it to the interstate and was picked
up by a trucker. His story pretty much ended there, as being
undocumented he wanted nothing to do with the police and

14

wasn't about to make an official report. I only heard about his terrifying tale and was able to talk to him because the guy who painted my house told me about it.

Nothing more was ever heard about the strange goings on at the remote trailer, at least nothing in the news I ever saw, but one has to wonder if the sect did eventually graduate to human sacrifice and murder. It was rumored that a deserted cabin was found out in that area containing the remains of four human bodies, at least the skulls arrayed in a warped display of some kind, but a subsequent search of newspaper and sheriff accounts contain no reference to it. Maybe they're still out there, holding their bloody orgies and fileting whatever unlucky hitch-hiker or victim they are able to procure? It wouldn't be the first or last time some blood cult has operated in the vast remoteness of the great Mojave and my files are filled with all sorts of stories and accounts from the late 1800's on till today. In the early days, finding headless bodies were attributed to various Native American attacks or renegades, but some whispered that the Black Mass were to blame. Often the newspapers of the time hinted at some sort of connection, but mainly treated it as just another desert mystery.

Take these two short articles from back in the day. This first one is from *The Sacramento Union* of November 21st, 1919, a date that puts it far after the subjugation of the indigenous people in the area and could only be attributed to the white man:

FIND HEADLESS BODY OF MAN ON DESERT

BAKERSFIELD, Cal. Nov. 20. - Though the officers investigating the finding of the headless body of a man in Red Rock canyon on the desert sixty miles from here have not yet returned, reports received here from them state that a knife and a half dozen revolver shells but no revolver, were found in the immediate vicinity of the body.

Not much to go on, just that someone took the poor guy's head after what seemed a short struggle. Rather strange behavior for a simple robbery or ambush don't you think? Here's another from the same paper, but four years earlier, *The Sacramento Union* of September 21^{rst}, 1914:

DEATH VALLEY CLAIMS FOUR WHO SEEK GOLD ONE DECAPITATED BODY FOUND IN DESERT

Special to the Union. TONOPAH (Nev.), Sept. 20. — That four prospectors, instead of one, have perished in the desert of Death Valley, is the belief of Sheriff Malley of this city and authorities of Inyo county, California. A report was recently brought to Rhyolite by two prospectors that the body of a man, with head and hands missing, supposedly eaten away by coyotes, had been seen near Stovepipe Wells, 35 miles from Rhyolite, in Inyo county. When Sheriff Malley communicated this information to Inyo county authorities he was informed that the dead man was believed to be one of a party of four prospectors, who recently left to prospect on and cross the desert together. Searching parties are being organized from both Tonopah and Inyo counties.

Now coyotes will eat the soft parts of a body, so the fact they might have been thought to have scavenged the hands comes as no surprise, but the head? No. They'll pull the body apart, but only after it has decayed and rotted. And they certainly wouldn't make off with just the head. But it's a fact that many cults are noted to have used the head and hands of their victims in gruesome alters and displays for their twisted ceremonies, so I would view this story as being a little more than first reported. A further search didn't yield any more articles on the case, but I did happen across an old tale about there being suspicions that "spiritualists linked to a dark organization" were at work in the desert at the time. I think we can all guess who these "spiritualists" were up to and what "dark organization" they were members of!

Perhaps one of the most famous later stories of a group of warped miscreants who really did murder and butcher people out in the desert (and elsewhere) is the tale of the Manson family and their "inspired" leader – Charles. Now I'm not sure whether to classify this under "blood cult" or simply "whacked out hippies who took too much acid" but their shocking murders and bloody crimes are a matter of public record and true enough.

Depending on who you ask, Charles Manson was either a highly intelligent man with a hypnotic personality or a failed musician who simply gathered feeble-minded and pathetic losers about him in a last attempt to gain some sort of fame and renown. His "brilliant" plan was to start a race war by killing innocent people, an idea he had concocted by dropping loads of LSD and listening to the Beatles' song

"Helter Skelter". Either way, he succeeded admirably, in murder at least, as his name is synonymous with a string of horrible and bloody deeds, the Tate-Labianca killings being the most famous. But Charlie and his little tribe of disheveled followers were also responsible for a string of killings of drifters and failed disciples, many of whose remote desert graves reportedly have yet to be discovered.

Mainly operating out of two remote areas – the Spahn movie ranch in Los Angeles county and the Barker Ranch out in the Mojave Desert in what is now the Death Valley National Park, the group were responsible for many tales of bloody mayhem. Although the most famous of their killings, the murder of actress Sharon Tate and her neighbors, took place back in 1969, the rumors of other murders having occurred out at their desert hideouts have persisted to this day. Enough so that in 2008, forensic investigators descended upon remote Barker Ranch with gear and cadaver sniffing dogs in an attempt to locate more graves. Nothing new was found, but a man who is familiar with the particulars of the search told me that is not too surprising as in his opinion the cadaver dogs are not too successful in practice most of the time. He personally had been on searches where the dogs raced right by a pile of rubble in which he could clearly see the remains of human bones. But this time in 2008, even with their modern electronics, the investigators turned up nothing worthwhile and the search was terminated and the tales of additional bodies basically considered folklore and myth.

But are they?

Central to the story is that Charles Manson and his followers had other isolated camps and spots out in the vast Mojave and it is there that the other killings, and yes, *sacrifices* were conducted. One of the more colorful and interesting of the stories is that the group had a passion for VW Beetle station wagons (what good hippies didn't?) and that their collection of the vehicles was provided by luring their drivers to these remote spots and killing them before burying their corpses way out in the surrounding desert. Manson would often use the young women who were under his thrall as sexual bait for many of his victims so it is not too surprising that horny male drivers would be up for a promised romp with the girls somewhere way off the main road. No other camping area has been officiated as being a certified Manson hangout, but an archeologist working for the BLM (Bureau of Land Management) told me off the record that while locating abandoned mine holdings he had personally stumbled across a site he was positive had been used by the group. He said there was graffiti on some of the rocks echoing the whole nutty "Helter Skelter" thing as well as curses and threats against "the pigs" that match up pretty well with the radical lingo of the era. He could also see where an old cabin or lean-to had been located, and a well-used, but old, fire ring built. Although I pointed out any of those things could have been the work of locals or drunk kids, he said most emphatically it was the overwhelming feeling of "pure evil" that pervaded the place that made him think it was legit.

"I've never had that feeling before," he told me, "at least not so strong. It was disturbing just to be there."

I asked if he reported it to his superiors, but he said they told him to not say anything about it or mark it on the survey as I assume they didn't want the hassle of having people try to make it out there and get in trouble rather than any malicious attempt at a cover-up. It takes time and money to launch a forensic investigation and without more concrete proof other than "it felt evil" I bet the BLM has better uses for their budget. But who knows? Everyone is positive there more than a few corpses from all eras moldering away in undiscovered graves out in the vast Mojave, so why couldn't a couple be from the hippie "race prophet" Charles Manson?

Now let us move on from bloody cults and the work of deluded humans to something that is related but wrought by the hand of nature – maybe. If you're a fan of cryptozoology, the study of unknown or "hidden" animals and beings, some from the natural world or others from folklore and ancient tales, then you know there is no shortage of strange flying creatures that have been seen and reported by people over the ages. Some, such as the infamous "Mothman" down in West Virginia have been credited with all sorts of strange and occult powers to accompany their nefarious activities, and out here in the Mojave we too have stories of "demonic" flying creatures who seem to delight in harming or menacing humans. Indeed; many of the Native American rock art sites that cover the Southwest depict all manner of strange winged creatures that are open to numerous theories of origin. While I could devote an entire book to their stories (and might at a later date) for this volume of Mojave Mysteries dealing with the lower part of the great desert in California, I'll stick to one of my favorites that I have some personal experience with; *The Demon Flyer*.

No, I've never seen it, but a couple I met on my travels through the Mojave National Preserve (an awesome expanse of three million acres of wilderness containing old mines, gorgeous vistas and plenty of wildlife) regaled me one night with their encounter with the winged monstrosity while sharing a campfire. I have been telling them of one of my own sightings of a flying curiosity, nothing spectacularly dramatic; just an albino bat that I had seen on two separate nights when the wife got all silent and gave her husband a look that I knew meant they too had a story. It took a little bit of pushing to get them to tell it, as they obviously thought I would consider them crazy, and both being professional photographers for numerous nature websites probably didn't want to risk their reputations. After making me promise I would never identify them by name if I ever recited it to others, they threw another log on the fire and started in on the tale.

Both had been out on assignment in Death Valley two winters previous taking pictures of the beautiful slot canyons up in the auspiciously named Owlshead Mountains. It was late in the day; the sun was almost behind the surrounding mountains and they were just getting ready to head back to camp for the night when the wife thought she saw a huge bird gliding on the wind between two ridges.

"What caught my eye," she said, "was the size. At first I thought it might be a condor, but the shape of its wings wasn't as square looking. More pointed and sharp."

Hoping to get a shot, she persuaded her husband to quickly pack his gear and they trudged over to the base of the tall rocky ridge where the "bird" was last seen. Arriving at the bottom of the ridge the first thing she noticed was that the rocks she had seen it glide behind were larger than expected, meaning the size of the thing must have been much bigger than she had first estimated.

"That kind of made a chill go down my spine, as it would mean the thing was like two or three times the size of a condor or hunting owl."

For the record, a California condor's wingspan can reach up to lengths of almost ten feet, so to be twice that size meant something huge.

"My husband said I must have seen its shadow on the ground (the sun was at its back) and mistaken it for the bird itself. I didn't think so."

Regardless, upon seeing no more of the mysterious flyer, they retired to their nearby SUV and made a fire in preparation of cooking some supper. They had one of those roof-top tents that allow you to sleep on the top of your vehicle, so after a meal and some time spent packing their camera gear for the morning's departure, the two climbed up and went to sleep.

"We were pretty fried from being out in the sun all day, so we went out like a light."

They had let their fire burn out before turning in and the night was now dark and silent.

"I'm not sure of the time, but I think around midnight I woke up because Tom (her husband) was snoring really bad and pushing me off my pad. I had just turned over and started poking him to wake up when I heard what sounded like a whooshing noise and suddenly the sound of the cooler being knocked over. We had left it on the hood so no coyotes would mess with it while we were asleep and I heard it clatter off pretty loud and hit the ground. That freaked me out because no coyote could get up that high and as far as I know there are no bears out there. I shook Tom, who also heard the clatter and we both sat up in the darkness and listened. It sounded like something was ripping into some of the food. We didn't have a gun or anything, just our flashlights so after a bit of whispering we decided to unzip the door, which was on the side the noise was coming from, and look out. We even counted like "one, two, three" before we did it. Being somewhat anxious, we only got it halfway down before the damn zipper caught on the fabric but even so we pulled the flap in and stuck our flashlights out to see. Down just in front of the right bumper I saw this weird black shape hunched over pawing at the food that was scattered out all over the ground. My first thought was "Oh my God, it is a bear!" when suddenly I saw it turn its head toward us and look over its left shoulder. I distinctly saw a head and a flash of its eyes before it just crouched down and suddenly leapt into the air while these two huge, and I mean huge "bat wings" unfolded and flapped hard until it was gone in the dark. The whole thing took like a few seconds and it was gone, just up, up and it was gone."

Her husband added his recollection. "I didn't see any head but definitely saw the wings when it jumped up and took off. All black. Rather rubbery looking. No feathers either. Definitely smooth like skin or something."

I asked him how big the thing was?

"Impressive. If I had to guess; I'd say the body was about the size of a large child or smallish human female. Didn't see any legs. At least nothing I could recognize as legs. My eyes were on those bloody great wings."

His wife finished the account.

"We flashed our lights all up in the air where it looked like it had gone, but didn't see anything. Looking at the ground we saw the food was tossed all over but nothing looked eaten. After that there was NO way I was staying up in that thin tent, so I made Tom sleep in the SUV with me and you can be sure we locked the doors! A couple of times I heard something and made him turn on the headlights and beep the horn, but we didn't see it again. In the morning, after a night of no sleep, we got out as soon as the sun was up and looked around. The food was all over and all the ice melted, but I was looking for tracks or anything that would show what it might have been. I didn't see anything other than a few long scratches on the ground where I thought it was crouching, but whether that was from the thing's feet or claws I couldn't say. We did take pictures of them though, not that you can see much. The hood had a couple good long scratches from the cooler being dragged off and when we returned the SUV the next day (it was a rental) the man at the tour place noticed them too. We just said our cooler was up there and got blown off in a wind. What were we going to say?"

I asked them if they ever saw the mysterious thing again and both said no. When I questioned the wife on what the "head" looked like, she couldn't give me much of a description. "It was large and tucked down into the shoulders. When it turned to look at us, the left shoulder blocked the lower half but I did see the face was flat and forward looking. And I did see eyes – they flashed a reddish glow like when you shine your flashlight at an animal in the dark. Really spooky. But the most shocking thing was just how big it was and how fast it moved when it wanted out of there. Just sat back and then jumped into the air. And those wings! We called it the "bat thing" and tried to figure out what it could have been, but there was nothing really we could pin it down to be. But we both saw it."

There wasn't much more to their story and I can only add that although the Mojave has plenty of bats, none come close to something that size. At least all the thing desired was whatever food was in the cooler and seemingly not interested in the couple sleeping in their roof-top tent. But what I wondered was this – did the thing smell the food, or had it been out in the darkness watching them the whole time and figured out that was where the grub was kept? Now *that* presents a more worrisome picture!

Having heard that story from the couple I did some research and tried to find out more about any sightings about such a creature or apparition. A few people told me they had heard about what they called "The Demon Flyer" but no one had seen it recently. A web search turned up lots of stuff about a "Demon Flyer" but most of it came from Papua, New Guinea of all places! About as far from Death Valley and the Mojave Desert as you can get. And the accounts seem to describe something more akin to a flying reptile than a giant bat or devilish hybrid. But then I got an email from a man who claimed he'd seen the thing up close and personal and gave me a good description. His email was rather verbose and rambling in spots, so I will distill it down to the pertinent facts and omit the extended account of his family and their history in the area. Suffice it to say they are from pioneer stock and his ancestors came into the area back in the late 1860's following the civil war.

"I was driving down Lost Section Road and it was just after dark. I was headed back to our cabin (we have grandfather rights to a plot) and was reaching down into a bag of nuts I had on the seat next to me when I seen it. At first I thought I was looking at the ass end of a big black dog eating something by the side of the road but when I got closer it stood up and looked right at me. I took my foot off the gas in shock and just kind of coasted past it as it looked at me. I say "it" but would you believe me if I told you it looked like a woman? A really scary devil-like woman! All black and leathery with red eyes. She hissed at me and then just as I got to near where she stood, she unflapped (sic) out these big wings and went almost straight up! Just took off! I tell you I hit the gas and didn't stop until I got back to the cabin and even then I grabbed the shotgun and went outside to make sure she hadn't followed me! Never saw her again, but I seen it that night. And no, wasn't drinking. It was looking right into my window and I seen it good. I told my wife's family about it but they don't like to talk about it as they are very religious and think it's the devil or one of his demons. One of them said she heard about something like that when she was a little girl raising up in the area and people said it would like to kill you if it ever got you out alone somewhere."

Now we all know when you're tired and on the road for a bit your eyes can play tricks on you, but this gentleman was adamant that he had seen the thing up close and personal and would not allow for any other interpretation. And when I queried him about how he knew it was a woman, his email reply was equally terse and certain.

"Seen the teets (sic). Was a woman alright. Nasty."

Well, that's about all the info I have on this flying nightmare, other than that some of the locals reportedly also call it the Demon Flyer and swear it haunts the ridge tops and roads in some of the remoter parts of the Owlshead Mountains. I'd love to meet up with some of the local tribes and see if they have anything like that in their mythology, but as of yet I have not made any contacts to do so.

Not much to go on, but whenever I get back out that way I want to be sure to take my expensive night vision scope and do some nocturnal spotting. Who knows, maybe someday the leathery gal will come flash her blazing red eyes at me too?

UFO's, Alien Encounters and Crashes

To many people, the desert is the place to see a UFO, and in some cases, their other-worldly "pilots". With its vast open horizons and often complete lack of light pollution, the night sky is visible like nowhere else. Astronomers flock to the desert to view the open heavens and almost all travelers and explorers can relate to the beautiful nights filled with endless displays of celestial wonder. And of course, with all those eyes turned skyward, someone is bound to see something strange. I myself have seen several things in the night sky that I could not readily identify, yet would be loath to automatically assign an extraterrestrial origin to them, as I know the military out here is constantly testing things we can only dream of. But many of the people in the stories I am about to relate harbor no such doubts, they're sure they have seen visitors from another world and even encountered them face to face.

Now by this stage of the game, almost everyone the world over knows and is familiar with the story of Roswell, New Mexico and the purported crash in 1947 of a "flying saucer". But how many have heard of the night a strange object came down near the small Mojave Desert town of Needles, California? It has all the same elements of the classic crash story – an unknown craft, military recovery activity, mysterious "men in black" and possible alien control.

It happened in May, 2008, down where the Colorado river winds its way along the California/Arizona border near the town. A large object said to be "the size of a semi-trailer" arced across the night sky emitting a turquoise glow, stalled for a moment then plunged to the ground. Seen by more than a few people in town, along the highway and out in the river itself, the object apparently made no noise and even stranger, didn't make a loud crash as it slammed into the ground. Thinking a small plane had crashed, several witnesses made calls to the local police department. Within minutes, it was also reported that a fleet of black helicopters appeared from the direction of Las Vegas to the north and descended upon the area where the object was thought to have crashed. For the record, the famed Area 51 is down near that end of Nevada and many UFO buffs have surmised the helicopters were a crash recovery team that was tracking the unknown craft and waiting to pounce on it once it dropped out of the sky. Among the choppers was reportedly a Sky-Crane, a model that can sling heavy objects underneath and it was to this helicopter that the unknown object was quickly fastened and soon on its way back north with the rest of the black fleet. Anyone venturing near the area was warned off.

Now since that day, the story has gone around and around that the whole thing was a hoax cooked up by the local radio station for some easy publicity or simply a large meteorite that briefly lit up the sky before breaking up (which would be pretty cool in itself). Some claimed the crash was of a new type of experimental unmanned spy plane or drone and that the military, not Area 51 spooks had been behind the recovery. A quick Google search of the story "Needles Ca UFO" will bring up a plethora of articles, both positive and negative, but the reason I have included the story here is because I heard about it from two people directly involved – a civilian contractor who does classified work for the U.S. Army and a man who was hunting in the area. What makes this an interesting mystery to me is that both men, who I like and consider sane and sensible, have two diametrically opposite takes on the same story.

My contractor friend never spills any secrets about what he does other than to say he designs highly sensitive micro-optics for surveillance drones, as he takes his oath very seriously. But when I mentioned to him I'd heard on the radio about a "crashed UFO in the Mojave" he laughed and said it was a drone test gone wrong as they are constantly testing the objects in a variety of conditions and "lose them all the damn time." When I asked him about it being "the size of a semi-trailer" he said that was ridiculous as the trend in drone technology is make them smaller and smaller, not the size of a damn truck. In his opinion, the story is literally a mountain made out of a molehill. While he wasn't on site, he said he knew for a fact that they had lost a drone in that area around that time and the activity people had witnessed must simply be a low intensity search and recovery effort by the drone team. To him, it's case closed.

But to my other friend, a man who loves to spend countless days in the wilderness and hunts all over the state, it was something else entirely. I'll give his name as Martin G. and let him tell it in his own words;

"I was hunting out across from an old jeep trail that straddles Big Wash near the hills. It was late, don't know the time but after midnight. I was finishing dressing the last of my rabbits when I heard something making a high-pitched whiney noise pass overhead. Looked up and way up there saw what looked like an oblong tear-dropped shaped thing, with sparks coming off it, shoot over me. It banked to the left as it went by and then pulled up, kind of shuddered a few times and dropped almost straight down behind a far ridge maybe a mile and half, two miles away. Didn't see or hear anything so don't know if it hit the ground or landed softly. The ridge was blocking my view. It was weird looking but as I was already running late and the wife was waiting, I just got washed up and planned on heading home as fast as I could.

Figured I'd read about in the papers later. I was too tired to really give a shit to be honest, I'd been out in that sun all day and was pretty beat.

I hopped in the truck and made my way back down the wash to where I could pick up the jeep trail again and head back to the power line road. It was rough as hell so it took me maybe three quarters of an hour to get to the trail and then another half hour to make the line road. I turned on it and headed south. I'd only gone about three miles when I saw two choppers cross over the road low and head back along the wash toward the ridge where I'd seen the thing drop. They only had their red running lights on and I couldn't see what type. Just saw them silhouetted against the sky when they popped up to cross the road. I kept going for another two miles when I rounded a corner and found the road blocked by two dark gray Hummers backed bumper to bumper and several guys carrying black rifles. They weren't wearing uniforms but looked military. Dressed tight and wearing caps. One of them waved at me with a flashlight and pointed for me to stop.

Rolling up, I leaned out and the guy came up and without asking me where I was going told me I'd have to turn around and go back the way I came. I asked why and he said "they" was working in the area and the road was closed. He wasn't shitty about it, just matter of fact. I got the vibe he was a cop or military police or something. There weren't any markings on the Hummers though and whole thing just seemed strange. But they had the hardware alright. I wasn't about to argue.

Now the problem was, I was low on gas and to go back down the power road and all the way over to where I could get to the highway was too far. Like three hours. I told him I'd run out of gas. He listened and had me show him my gas gauge, then stepped away and talked to someone on his radio. They were wearing those chest rigs with the walkie-talkie or whatever strapped to their shoulder. After a few minutes, he came back and told me to turn off the engine and someone would be up to take care of me. He kept calling me "sir" and was polite so I didn't take it as a threat. I waited. For the next twenty minutes I smoked a cigarette and sat in the truck. The soldiers or guards or whatever stood around chatting and hanging back by the Hummers. I saw there was at least six of them. Finally, I saw a pair of bright headlights cross out of the wash behind me onto the road and come speeding up to where we were. It was another Hummer, same gray paint. It pulled up behind me. A guy got out of it and went around to the back. I got out as the one guy who did all the talking came back over to my truck. He said "we'll fix you up" and nodded to the Hummer behind me. Sure enough here comes the other guy with two five-gallon fuel cans in his hands. He stops and without a word screws on the nozzle and starts dumping it into my truck. I asked the first guy if they were Army and he shook his head and turned away. Like I said, he wasn't shitty about things, but I distinctly got the feeling that asking too many questions was not the thing to do. After a few minutes and both cans he looked at me and said "you can get going now, have a good night."

That was it. I got in, turned around and headed back down the line road. I looked in the rearview and saw the men were all standing there by the Hummers watching me so I gunned it and put some miles between us. Nothing else happened but when I finally got to the end of the line road and started toward the highway I saw two chopper gunships come over from the north and heading back toward the area where I saw the thing fall. It was dawn and I could clearly see them in the sky. When I got home I told the wife before she went to work. A couple days later we heard on the radio that people had seen a UFO and said it crashed on the west side of the river. I guess I must have seen it and that was what those guys were out "working on". Wish now I'd gone over that ridge and had a look but it would have been too far - or maybe not, they were nice enough but I wouldn't have wanted to piss them off. Not with everyone carrying so much hardware."

Now this sounds like it could pretty much be in accord with my contractor buddy saying it was a simple drone test gone bad, but it's what happened next to Martin that makes it really strange.

"For the next few weeks everyone was talking about the "UFO that crashed" but no one really knew anything and I had only told my wife about my run in with the Hummer guys. Then one day she got home from work and told me that someone had called their office (she's in real estate) and wanted to verify that I was her husband? They used my full name including my middle name. The manager told the person I was and then later she told my wife about the call. Then the next day I got a call on my cell from an unknown number and when I answered it there was just a clicking sound and then it hung up. This happened two days in a row, and at all times of the day or night. I would have figured it was just some bullshit marketing robo-call thing, but it was what happened on the weekend that really got me worried.

I went back out hunting, not in the same spot I saw the thing go down, but maybe ten miles away on the opposite side of the line road. I left my truck in a sandy wash and went off on foot and was gone maybe three or four hours. When I got back to my truck I instantly noticed that there was another set of tire tracks right next to my truck. Boot prints showed that two people got out and walked all around my truck. I also saw that there were small chunks of fresh white plaster near the right front tire and the weirdest thing – someone had circled one of my boot prints in the sand and put an arrow pointing toward it! I was kind of stressed out and after making sure there was no one around, I jumped in and headed back to town. Sure enough, when I got to the highway and rolled into town I was going past the Shell station and what do I see? Two of those gray Hummers parked side by side in the dirt lot behind! The windows were blacked out so I couldn't tell if anyone was in them. I thought about pulling in and driving by them but to tell the truth, I was feeling a little bit anxious and just wanted to get home to tell my wife. We both agreed it was strange.

I didn't really know what to make of the whole thing, but on that Monday I was back on the job and talking to a friend of mine I was doing some electrical work for. I told him about the Hummers and then the tracks by my truck. He said that lots of people had been talking about some guy who'd seen the UFO and called it in, but was now missing. He lived on a houseboat on the river and no one had seen him since. He also said that whomever had rolled up on my truck and left the plaster and marks must have been getting my tire tracks and boot prints. Why, I asked? "To see if you were near that thing probably" was his response. Now that was a kick! Made me pretty paranoid. Would they really do that? On the way home I went past the Shell station again but didn't see any Hummers, but I was sure looking for them. Over the next few weeks I was super worried about the whole "getting my prints thing". Even stopped hunting for a few months because I didn't want to go back out there alone in case I ran into those guys. Luckily, I didn't get any more "click" calls and in the fall, I started going back out hunting, but kept well away from the area where I'd seen the thing fall. Never found any more tracks near mine, so I guess they forgot about me, but I still wonder if I'm on file somewhere?"

So, there you have Martin's take on the story. If you search for the Needles UFO you'll get all sorts of opinions, but these are the only two people I heard it from in person. UFO or errant drone? Men in Black or Men in Gray? Radio hoax or brush with the bizarre or possibly even extraterrestrial? The only thing for sure is it's a neat little story that goes into the file labeled Mojave Mysteries.

Now if we travel to the huge expanse of desert known as Death Valley we will find more accounts of crashed UFOs and their occupants as well as mysterious lights in the sky. The first case I've discovered was from 1949, when two prospectors named Mace Garney and Buck Fitzgerald gave an interview to *The Bakersfield California*, a small regional paper, in which they recounted a story of having seen a "flying saucer" crash while out working claims near the searing dunes just north of the justly named Furnace Creek. The men claimed a shining metal disk, twenty-four feet in diameter and moving at an estimated speed of three hundred miles an hour zoomed over them before slamming into the soft desert floor a short distance away. Running over to see the object, both men were amazed to see two small occupants, described as "humanoid and dwarf-like" crawl out of the mostly-intact wreckage and upon seeing the approaching prospectors run off into the desert. The men gave chase for a short distance before losing sight of them among the twisting dunes, when suffering from the effects of the intense heat both prospectors gave up the pursuit and returned to examine the strange craft.

And there the story ends.

Both men claimed to the paper that they had measured the craft and then set off for civilization to report their incredible experience. No further search was mounted for the crashed saucer or its wayward occupants as I gather the authorities were not exactly impressed by the veracity of the two prospectors. In any case, no trace of a crashed ship was ever found in that area and the story was soon forgotten, being no doubt chalked up to too much celebratory whiskey and fevered imagination. Still, I like the image of two grizzled prospectors running after the small alien pilots as they bound over rock and scrub in a desperate attempt to escape after having put their flying saucer in the ditch like a couple of buzzed teenagers.

Now a tale that has a bit more of a sinister and spooky twist involving strange lights in the sky comes from the long stretch of dirt track that leads into the southern portion of Death Valley, a remote trail known as Saratoga Springs road. In 1977 a woman driving down the road at night reported an encounter that terrorized her for years. I heard about it from her daughter, who on account of the more salacious aspects of the story wanted her and mother's names kept out of this book. I'll just refer to her as "Helen" and this is her story:

"My mother only told me this after my father died and she had been diagnosed with breast cancer. I guess she felt the end was coming and she wanted to tell someone. She was a very religious person, so I couldn't imagine why she would tell me such a thing unless it was true.

Anyway, she said one night in 1977, winter, she was coming down Saratoga Springs to go to the hardware store down in Baker to fetch some things my dad needed on the ranch (they had a small holding since purchased by the park service). She was going to spend the night at her sister's in Baker and go to the hardware the next morning before coming back. It was about nine o'clock at night and mom said she was just driving along when she saw a flashing light way down the road ahead. It was very bright and looked to be red and blue. Thinking it was probably a sheriff's truck she slowed down and looked ahead for some type of accident or crash. Everyone used to drive that road so fast because it's just country and often there were wrecks. Sometimes they wouldn't be found for days.

As she came closer to the light she said it got so bright she slowed down because she almost couldn't see the road. All of a sudden the light stopped, just went out, and at the same time her car stalled. Just quit running. The headlights stayed on but the car just slowed and rolled to a stop in the middle of the road. She tried several times to start it, but it would just grind like the starter was dead. She was looking down at the keys as she turned and turned them, but when she looked up she suddenly saw someone standing in the road just at the edge of her lights. It was just a shadow but she thought it might have been a sheriff's deputy coming to help. But then, and this is where she said she would have liked to have had a heart attack, she saw there was *someone* standing right next to the car, right at her window! She screamed 'cuz it scared her so. The figure was tall and she could only see him from the waist up, mostly just a black outline. Then he put his hand on the window and she could see it was really long and pale, the skin looking like a lizard's belly or something, just scaly and terrible. Then she passed out, or at least can't remember anything much. She said it felt like she was dying 'cuz she just couldn't move a muscle or even scream.

When she woke up or could remember anything she said she was slumped forward in the car, still sitting in the middle of the road but with the engine now running and the headlights still on. There didn't seem to be anyone around, but her side window was down and she could smell the creosote bushes outside the car. Then she noticed her dress was unbuttoned almost to her waist and her shoes were on the seat next to her! The poor thing also said she had messed herself, most likely from fear. I certainly would have.

Anyway, after a few minutes, she put the car back in drive and started slowly down the road. She said it took her a few minutes to remember where she was and where she was going. She thought about turning around and going home, but for some reason just kept driving. She also didn't want to get out of the car and clean herself or put her shoes back on, just had the feeling she had to keep moving. Then after about ten minutes or so, she said she heard a loud humming noise and something huge zoomed over the car and down the road in front of her. It was flashing red and blue again and by the time she could see it, the light just stopped dead for a second and then shot straight up into the sky and was gone. Just vanished in the blink of an eye! When she finally got down to Baker an hour later, she said she just burst into her sister's house crying and wanting to throw up. She couldn't explain what happened and felt like someone had "touched her" in a sexual way. She ended up spending a week down there and told my dad, who was concerned and also mad about not getting his tools, that she had got the stomach flu and couldn't come home yet. Eventually she drove back, but said she did it in the middle of the day and even then was almost crying with fright. She never drove that road again at night and certainly never told my dad or anyone, including me, until she was old and sure the end was coming. Oh, and she never found any marks on her body but did say the car window had an oily smudge on it that never really washed off."

Whoa! Now that story would have had me shaking too. I asked Helen if her mom ever told her exactly what she thought the encounter was, but all she said that was being a very religious woman, her mom speculated that it might have been something demonic rather than extraterrestrial. I can't say I've heard of too many demons zooming about old dirt roads with flashing lights stopping cars, but I wasn't there so can only relate what I was told. But that would have had me watching the sky for sure.

Some of the other reports I've come across of UFO's and strange lights seen in the California section of the Mojave over the years come from a desolate range of rugged mountains down near what is now the western section of Joshua Tree National Park. They are called the Coxcombs, and aside from being remote and full of some spectacular rock formations and peaks, have an interesting pedigree and history. Now technically this area is right on the transitional border between the Mojave and Colorado desert ecosystems, but as this dividing line is rather fluid and not something that is etched in stone I am including these stories in this California volume as well.

Early traders moving through the area back in the early 1800's often mentioned seeing lights glowing or flickering in the peaks while traveling past, but with no other information available we could probably put that down to being the fires or torches of native hunters going about their business. The real bit of high strangeness begins in the late 1940's, at a time when the news of Roswell and flying saucers was all the rage in the popular media. People were seeing them everywhere, but it wasn't until a man named George Adamski claimed he had actual contact with the alien pilots that the modern era of the "contactee" was ushered in.

And where did Adamski say he first met with his alien friends?

The Coxcombs!

Adamski claimed that in 1952, after years of seeing strange flying objects in the skies of southern California, he was driving with some friends through the desert out by the eastern slope of the Coxcombs when they spotted a large UFO in the distance. Feeling the object was somehow "looking for him", he followed it out into the open desert and parked. Telling his rather startled companions to wait for him, he hiked out into the base of the Coxcombs and was gone for several hours. Upon returning, Adamski claimed he had indeed found the UFO landed, and was able to converse with its pilot, a being named "Orthon" who declared he was from Venus and had important information to impart. This "alien" was reported to have long flowing hair, a well-tanned skin and was tall and thin. He also wore strange trousers and had boots that left mysterious symbols imprinted on the ground. I won't regurgitate all the details as a simple Internet search will give you all the info but let's just say it reads like a bad 1950's science fiction movie. Adamski claimed he often met with the aliens, took rides in their spaceships and saw all kinds of fantastic things (like cities and lakes on the far side of the moon) and today is pretty much considered a complete crank. In later years, he also stated he had met secretly with the Pope on orders from the extraterrestrials and was awarded a special medal by the Pontiff for his efforts in securing an understanding between them, but as to what the details were he never really answered. He died in 1965 while still on the UFO lecture circuit. Although his stories were pretty laughable, I do find it fascinating that he decided to claim the Coxcombs as the spot where aliens came to interact with humans, as several other famous UFO stories also come from the desert surrounding the range.

Just thirty miles back from where Adamski was meeting with "Orthon" that year, a man named Barry Storm was working a jade mine he claimed had been shown to him by three flying saucers beaming a light down onto a small hillock. Storm swore that UFO's had also guided him in his wanderings and the fact is he actually found something! His small open mine is still there for all visitors to Joshua Tree National Park to see if they want to make the hike out to it. I have detailed its location and fascinating history later in this book.

The other story about UFO's in the Coxcombs is one I got from an older rancher when I first moved to the high desert. He is now in a retirement home and reaching the end of the line, but his mind is still sharp and he remembers all the details of that one scary night, having related it to me many times. In 1962 he was working with the road crew then tasked with widening the shoulders on an old water district road that soon became California State Route 177, the thin strip of pavement that skirts along the eastern part of the Coxcombs and connects Highway 62 to the lower I-10. It's a pretty desolate bit of country now, but back in the 1960's it was downright lonely. The men would spend the day out in the sun using their graders and trucks, then knock off around four o'clock in the afternoon. All the heavy earth-moving equipment would be parked in a small spot and left overnight until the crew returned at the crack of dawn the next day to resume work. Since the rancher also happened to work as a mechanic for the county, he would sometimes drive himself to the site (most of them car-pooled from town) and stay late to work on any of the equipment that needed field repairs. And so, it was one hot night in June that he was working on a dozer when it happened:

"It was about ten o'clock and I was trying to pry a link in a cat track together so I could put in the connecting pin. I was using a piece of heavy metal railing to pry the links together and cussing a storm when I heard, or felt, this low rumble. At the same time, I saw a big shadow, like a cloud start to pass over and block the moonlight from above. It was almost full that night and there were a few clouds in the sky so I thought it was just one of them drifting by. But the sound got louder and I could even feel it vibrating the bar in my hand so I levered it back and looked up. Right above me cruising over was this big black triangle shaped thing! It wasn't making any noise other than that low rumble and didn't have no lights on it. Just looked like a giant kid's kite about a couple hundred feet off the ground sailing along toward the mountains. I watched it for a few minutes till it angled up and disappeared behind the peaks and was gone.

I didn't know what it was, but since it was gone and it was late I went back to work. But the second I grabbed the bar again and put it in the track I got one hell of a shock! Like when you wear your socks on the carpet and touch a doorknob, like that, but ten times worse! Made me jump back and yell. I noticed the hair on my arms was standing up and I felt all prickly and funny. That was it; I decided to call it a night and head back. I jumped in the truck and was just stepping on the starter when I looked out the window and damn if this thing ain't coming back nearly right along the same path! I stomped the starter but it just groaned and wouldn't start. Pretty soon the damn thing is almost right above me again, but this time off to the side a bit so I can get a look at how thick it was. If I had to eyeball a guess, I would say it was about thirty feet thick and about the length of two city buses and all solid black. No lights, no markings, nothing. Just sailing along like you please except for that low rumble. When it got a way off I was able to start the truck and took off out of there for home.

Next day I come back and nothing was different or disturbed. I got the business alright for not having finished repairing the track, but standing there in the daylight surrounded by my boss and crew, I decided not to say nothing and let it go. But you can be sure I never went out alone at night the rest of the job to fix nothing – oh, and that day we had to jump every battery on the graders and dozers to get them started, all were dead so whatever that rumble was, it had something to do with electricity. Drained every damn one of them."

Strange, but such accounts really should come as no surprise to anyone familiar with this particular area. One has to only search the internet for a short time to find page after page of people's accounts of UFOs or aliens that they have seen in the Mojave near Joshua Tree National Park and the surrounding desert going back to the late 1940's. For example, just outside the park up in Landers (a very small community just to the north of Joshua Tree) there stands Giant Rock, an iconic spot to many UFO devotees and fans of alien contact. It is just as its name suggests – a single giant boulder (like seven stories high) sitting on a flat expanse of sandy desert floor in the middle of nowhere. Originally a sacred spot to the Native Americans that inhabited the area for the past thousand years, it is now more associated with ufology and paranormal researchers. This is mainly because of one man, George Van Tassel, an interesting if rather eccentric individual who was at one time a top-flight inspector and mechanic for Hughes Aircraft. If you Google his name you will see his long and interesting history, but the short version is that he became convinced he had been visited by aliens while staying out at Giant Rock and spent the rest of his life running a small airport and holding UFO conventions there, as well as also building the "Integratron", a domed wooden building that was supposed to have healing and rejuvenation abilities provided one stood under its rotating mantel and received the powerful rays it produced. Apparently, the aliens gave Van Tassel the information to build the strange structure telepathically, and then only in short dribs and drabs so that it remained unfinished upon his death in 1978 and his heirs were unable to finish the project as they understandably had no blueprints to work from. The structure still stands by the way, and visitors can receive a healing "sound bath" after paying a small fee to the current owners. The whole story is quite fascinating, but as it stands outside my own personal experiences, I shall leave it with the observation that the whole high desert down there is thoroughly soaked in the lore of flying saucers and alien contact, so it's not too surprising that many visitors to Joshua Tree National Park and its surrounding environs swear they have seen and experienced UFO encounters. A simple web search will bring up a good helping of accounts if you plan on visiting the park.

I'll end this chapter with one of my own "mysterious" encounters, one that I don't assign any alien connection to, but none the less have no clue as to what I really saw. In May of 2004 I was camped out near the Old Woman Mountains in the lower eastern quadrant of the great Mojave about fifty miles from the Arizona border. The area is remote with just a few powerline roads running through it, but numerous mine and jeep trails to explore (and get lost on if you're not careful). At that time of year, the days can be nice and warm but the nights sometimes can be quite cold and chilling. I had a small jeep camp going, meaning my vehicle and my folding cot set up next to it. I rarely use a tent and like a lot of desert rats just carry a folding cot to throw out whenever I stop for the night in a remote area if traveling by jeep. When backpacking I just sleep on the ground or up in the rocks off the desert floor (depends on the snake, scorpion and tarantula population in the area).

I had finished my dinner, let the fire burn down and was laying on my cot wrapped in my warm blankets just watching the sky and enjoying life. One of my little hobbies is looking for satellites and with the lack of light pollution and open expanses in the Mojave you can usually see them as they flash and endlessly cross the night sky at all hours. In our modern world of electronics and telecommunications we have literally filled the sky with these objects (not to mention what the military throws up there) and there are even apps now for your phone that will tell you where and when to look, as well as what type of satellite you're seeing. That said, I still find it fun to just kick back and "see what I can see". This particular night I was laying there and just about to fall asleep when I noticed three small lights flying along in a perfect triangle formation start to come over the far horizon. They were no more than pin-points of light and at first I thought it was a plane or solid object of some sort. Grabbing my binoculars, I watched as they came over head, still very high up, and could now see that they were indeed separate lights as I could plainly see the other stars behind and between them as they moved silently along. Not too strange a thing at first, as I know there was a French company that uses three satellites in just such a formation to make highly accurate maps and was at the time sure that was what I was then seeing.

Then they broke apart and all started going in different directions!

And not smooth, even trajectories either. One kept on its original course, another pulled a super-fast 180 degree turn and started going back the way they had come, and the third one, strangest of all, started this bizarre falling leaf type pattern as it seemingly plummeted out of control. I watched all three, shifting my gaze from one to the other as they sped along. The first one just kept moving straight never deviating from its original path. The second, the one that had turned, now sped toward the opposite horizon at an incredible speed while the third one just made larger and larger z-shaped paths as it swung back and forth like someone swinging a lantern. Amazed, I watched as the two "flying" ones made it to their respective horizons and disappeared, and the "falling" one eventually just faded out, like a flare that had used up its fuel. Weird.

I wasn't then, and even more so now, sure of what I'd seen that night out in the Mojave. The one that kept moving was nothing spectacular, but the one that made the high-speed turn must have pulled some incredible g-forces to make such a violent move. And they were moving very fast, as the whole formation had crossed the entire visible sky in a matter of perhaps thirty seconds. And what about the third light? The one that was falling like a leaf? I have no clue what that could have been as it was moving right along in formation with the other two before it started its bizarre behavior and was not ejected or dropped by one of the others like a flare would be. I have no clue what they could be, but if I had to bet money on it I would say it was something military rather than extraterrestrial. My "company" friend, the military contractor I mentioned at the beginning of this chapter said after I related the story that he would bet it was yet another drone test, as no pilot in a manned vehicle could have survived so radical a maneuver at those speeds. And the falling one? "Probably a failure," he said, "it happens all the time".

I guess that brings us full circle in this chapter, but believe me, my files are filled with stories of UFOs and aliens in the Mojave and will publish more in future volumes.

The Cement Monster, Yucca Man and other Hairy Hominids

The idea that some large hairy man-like creature could be running about the United States undiscovered and cataloged by this late date would seem like a complete scientific absurdity. Yet, people still report them, find unexplainable large tracks or even more unsettling; interact with them on a regular basis. And to discover that out here in the vast Mojave Desert we have numerous and varied accounts of their presence would seem like the ultimate folly, but it happens! I myself have even found and photographed strange prints of enormous size and can offer no reasonable explanation of their origin as much as I tried. Which leads one to chuckle at the popular internet meme about "I'm not saying it was Bigfoot, but it *had* a big foot!" – until they of course experience it for themselves, or hear it from others who have.

It might surprise readers to learn that the various Native American tribes of the Mojave and surrounding areas have a rich lore and legacy of seeing and living with hairy man-like creatures. Everyone from the Apache to the Yuma tribes have seen and recorded their experiences throughout the centuries and one might still find their fascinating rock art showing depictions of "The Hairy Man", "Elder Brother" or "Yucca Man" on boulders and sheltered caves all over the desert. Often described as a being who lives between the worlds and only makes his (or her) presence known when they want to convey a message or teach a lesson, the hairy one also enjoys a far more sinister reputation. In some areas, he is called "The Man Stealer", not for any romantic inclination, but because he is a bloodthirsty cannibal who feasts on the lone hunter or snatched child with ghoulish relish. Indian mothers used to scare their children into behaving with admonitions that the hairy man would come get them if they were not good, much like modern mothers in the not too distant past would employ the boogie man to enforce discipline (before taking your video games away became the best way to get a kid's attention).

But what about the "modern" sightings and interactions with these strange hirsute creatures, do they also have a spiritual or teaching aspect to them? Well, not so much. It seems to modern eyes the hairy ones are much more circumspect and wary in their interactions and often with good cause; we have guns and drive fast powerful vehicles that make ending up as giant road kill a very real possibility. But yet the big man still likes to pop up in the most unlikely places and cause all sorts of reactions from fascination to outright fear and terror.

Let me share a few stories I have researched or discovered in my numerous desert travels.

The first one is a character that became known locally in the desert near Johnson Valley, California as "The Cement Monster" a name that has to be one of the feeblest and lamest monikers for a creature ever. I mean, who would fear being chased or menaced by something made out of concrete? Well, he wasn't and there is a quite understandable and reasonable origin to the name.

But first, a little background.

Highway 247 snakes along through a section of the Mojave from Barstow down to Yucca Valley, a section of rough and rugged land known as the high desert because of its elevation in relation to the nearby Coachella Valley (yes, that one where the annual music festivals are held). Mostly open ground dotted with a few rugged mountain ranges, the highway is the main corridor for traffic through the Lucerne Valley. And it was here, just past the small "town" of Lucerne that the Cement Monster was encountered. There is a long stretch of fairly remote highway that crosses the lower part of the valley although today it has much more rural development than it did in the heyday of the creature, which was in the 1970's and 1980's. At that time people were reporting a strange man-like beast they would catch glimpses of, mainly at night, while driving the lonely stretch of road or nearby intersecting Highway 18.

Described as being like a "huge prehistoric man" or "shaggy naked ape" (*not sure how you can be shaggy and naked at the same time, but okay…*) the Cement Monster would be seen darting across the road in front of startled drivers or creeping up on people if they stopped late at night to relieve themselves or change a blown tire. And this right in the area where an old cement factory stood abandoned in the nearby hills. At least at the time it was abandoned, today it is once again in full production, but then it was an open compound of empty industrial buildings and fenced off properties with only an occasional security patrol or watchman to keep the vandals away. It was here that the monster was most often seen by people, hence his name - The Cement Monster.

But slow and cumbersome he wasn't! Often the beast was just glimpsed as an approaching pair of headlights would pick out his large frame in mid-step while crossing the highway and then the giant form would take off in a fast leap and be gone into the darkness of the surrounding desert. I say "beast" but as stated, eye-witnesses often described him as looking much more human than animal, abet covered in hair and with the build of an Olympic weightlifter. One of the few actual eye-witness accounts I uncovered was by two off-duty Marines returning to their base in Twentynine Palms, California after spending the day skiing up in the mountains near Big Bear, a small resort town in the San Bernardino National Forest. The quickest way back to the base was along the highway that crosses the desert near Lucerne, and it was along this route, just past the old cement factory where the two off-duty soldiers saw it. As they slowed to make the turn onto highway 247, something very large seemed to stand up on two legs and begin crossing the road in front of them. Their headlights illuminated the thing from the ground to mid-waist, as they estimated it to be about eight feet tall. Covered in hair and with arms pumping like a sprinter, the "monster" ran in their headlights for a distance of about 150 feet before crossing the road in three great leaps and continuing on through the brush and scrub toward the factory. Amazed at what they were seeing, and being confident young Marines in fighting trim, they decided to give chase and turned down the lonely dirt road (now paved and lit) that led directly to the factory in an effort to either head the thing off or catch another glimpse of it. Arriving near the gates they looked around for a bit but the elusive man beast never reappeared, so they finally gave up and drove off. About the only real description of the thing they could offer up was that other than its huge bulk and height, it reminded them of "some sort of prehistoric man" and looked "monstrous". Interestingly enough, they also stated they would love to see the monster again as it was such an amazing experience.

Now the next witness to see the creature probably would not agree with the young Marines about ever wanting to encounter the Cement Monster again, as his experience was considerably more terrifying. John R., a lifelong resident of the Lucerne Valley lived alone in a small trailer just off highway 247, on a dirt road that crossed the Eastern side of the valley and headed towards Cougar Buttes. The Buttes are a concentration of soaring rock formations that house many a cave and lofty hiding spot, and figures prominently in the story of the Cement Monster.

Being home alone one night in the fall of 1987, watching his television and enjoying a late-night snack, John said his attention was diverted from the flickering screen when he saw an immense shadow cross by the window opposite him and at the same time heard something "really heavy" step up onto the flimsy wooden porch he had erected outside his front door. Not sure who would come calling at such a late hour and in such a remote spot, he immediately muted the television and grabbed his old shotgun, which like many deep desert dwellers he kept loaded and ready for action should anyone decide to drop in and "cause any shit". Listening intently, John heard the intruder step back off the porch and walk along the side of the trailer, their heavy footsteps crunching on the gravel in a steady bipedal gait. Next he caught the sound of the one of the big garbage cans he kept at the back of his property being overturned and decided it was time to grab the flashlight and have a look.

"I didn't have no yard light," he said, "just my big old metal Rayovac flashlight my old man had given me years before."

So, armed with his shotgun and light, John R. decided to first peer out the side kitchen window before heading out to confront the visitor:

"Couldn't see nothing out the kitchen, but I could sure hear the cans getting rolled and moved around so I decided to quietly open the door and have a look. If I knew then what the hell it was, you bet your ass I'd stayed put, that's for sure!

I let the latch off quiet as I could and let the door swing open a bit. I had the shotgun in one hand and the flashlight in the other so I just nudged the door with my foot until it was open enough that I could lean out and see toward the back of my trailer. It was night and pretty dark, but from the light coming from the kitchen window I could see something big and furry grubbing around in the garbage spilled from the cans. At first I thought *damn, that is one big bear!* People don't think we get bears out here in the desert, but being so close to the mountains, we sometimes get them coming down on their way to find food or get away from the fires if there's a blaze. I've personally seen three in my lifetime out here, just black bears, but they can go as large as three hundred pounds but they're usually pretty skittish and don't want no trouble.

Anyway, just as I was standing there wondering if I should put a charge of bird shot in this thing's ass, it turned around and stood up.

On two feet.

My first thought was that it was some guy in a puffy jacket or something and I popped on the flashlight and shown it right at him. Mother of God, if you'd seen the size of that son of a bitch! He was all chest and arms, covered in long brown hair and eyes reflecting back red as tail lights. I couldn't really see his face too good, as when I shined the light on him he quickly threw up his right hand to cover his face and let out a growl that damn near had me shitting in my pants. I mean it was loud! I could feel it beating on my chest. He definitely was letting me know he wanted no part of that light and me disturbing his dinner. I wanted to scream and drop dead, didn't even think about trying to get my gun on him. I was frozen. But before I could even take another breath, he hunkered right down like a sprinter and then just took off into the desert like a shot. I mean he was moving! Went straight out from my trailer and was gone before I could even swing the light to follow him. Not that I planned on doing that after hearing that growl. I was shaking. Finally, I got up the nerve to shine the light around and see if he was still out there, but thank God I saw nothing. My property is pretty open and he just seemed to melt back into the night as I never saw a thing after that. I went back inside and locked the door as quick as I could. Thought I was going to have heart attack. Must have smoked five cigarettes in row before I could calm down. I thought about calling the sheriff, but what was I going to say? Some hairy son of a bitch was eating my trash? And that was what he was doing alright, because in the morning after I came out having spent the whole night at the kitchen table with the lights on, I saw he had been rooting around in some rotten chicken I'd thrown out. Bet he got a bellyache from that! Least I hope he did. I sure didn't want that thing coming back."

John said he tried to see any tracks in the day light, but as the ground near his trailer is mainly gravel and pebbles, he couldn't find anything other than a few indentations where the thing had sprinted off upon being discovered. He's lived there ever since but had no more sightings of the creature. Talking with some of his "neighbors", the nearest house then being a good half mile away, no one said anything about seeing such an animal. It wasn't until a few years later he heard the name "Cement Monster" and read about some people seeing something similar out on the highway nearby. The only other thing he could remember about the sighting other than the sheer size of the "animal" was its hand. "Like a damn boat paddle," he recalled, "covered his whole face."

Now I do have one other eye-witness account where the person saw the creature's face in good detail, and that comes from 1977, quite a bit earlier than most of the stories I discovered when researching the Cement Monster, but it's worth recording. As anyone who's traveled across the desert knows, there can be long distances between facilities, and if one has to make a "pit stop" it usually means pulling off and using the nearest bush, pile of rocks or cactus for cover while so engaged. I can't tell you the number of vehicles I've come across stuck in the soft sand on the shoulder of a lonely road because the driver was trying to find a place to do his or her business, but it's certainly more than a few. Now if you're a man, it's not that big a deal, but for the ladies it can be a bit more involved, and this story deals with a woman who had to finally pull over and "water the cactus" after being on the road through the Lucerne Valley late at night.

Mary D. had been coming down from the town of Barstow to her mother's house in Flamingo Heights, a high desert settlement about ten miles past where the old cement factory stood. She volunteered her story one night at a party after she heard I was writing a book about weird stuff in the desert:

"I'd been driving since midnight because I wanted to get there before my mom left for work in the morning. I'd been drinking coffee like crazy to stay awake and had to go to the bathroom really bad. There's nothing between Barstow and Lucerne and by the time I got there the only gas station was closed and back then there wasn't much else at the crossroads. I thought I could make it to her house but finally just past the factory turnoff (*Note - Camp Rock Road if you're ever out that way*) I had to pull over. There hadn't been any cars on the road for a while, I think it was probably about two in the morning, so I decided to just go to the other side of my car and squat down.

So there I was, doing my thing, when I heard like a low grunt or cough right behind me. I turned around and right there, standing directly behind me about ten feet away was this huge shape! I first thought it was some hitchhiker or someone out on the road. I almost fell over pulling up my pants as fast as I could and trying to turn around and see who it was at the same time. I had left the car running and lights on, so I could see him totally lit up by the back lights, so he was in a totally red glow. At first I thought it was some guy in a long fur coat but then I could see he was like hairy, all over, just covered in long stringy hair. It reminded me of my horse's mane, really coarse and wavy. I couldn't tell what color or anything, because like I said, the tail lights were making everything all red. I screamed go away or something like that but don't really remember. He just stood there looking at me and then down at the puddle in the dirt I'd made. Then he kind of leaned in and I saw his face really good through his bangs. He looked human but with real big jaws and a funny nose, kind of small and mushed in. I saw him crinkle it like he was smelling or something. I thought he was going to jump on me or something but he just stood there and I just dove into the passenger side, it wasn't locked, and tried to get into the driver's seat and take off. I was crying by this time and freaking out. I actually knocked it out of gear turning the steering wheel wildly as I tried to get back on the road and the engine made a huge roar. I think it might have scared him because when I looked in the mirrors I couldn't see him anywhere and when I got it back in drive I totally gassed it to get out of there. It was really dark and that was all I ever saw. My hands were shaking so hard and I was crying the whole way down to my mother's. When I got there I woke her up and told her but she didn't know what to say, but was concerned I was having a breakdown or something. Yeah, a breakdown alright! I never told anyone until a few years ago when I saw some old article on the web about "The Cement Monster" and found out other people had seen it too. It's been so long now that I'm not really scared thinking about it, because he didn't really try to hurt me or anything. But it was the last thing a gal wants to see when she's trying to have a pee!"

Well I guess we can add "voyeur" to the hairy guy's resume along with sprinter and garbage raider, but at least he never seemed really interested in hurting anybody. And what about anyone that actually worked at the cement factory itself? Did they ever see or hear anything at the time the monster was out and about? I've only ever heard from two men that claimed to be employed as part-time security guards at the abandoned plant during the time, and then only by short email. One said he thought the whole thing was a "load of shit" made up by bored locals (although that doesn't account for people that were just driving through and reported seeing the thing) but the other, as typical in so many of these cases, had quite the opposite opinion. He said that often he would see footprints, "large bare foot prints" in the dirt along the barb wire of the fencing, and find where someone or something, had pushed the wire down and continued on into the mix area as though searching for something. Garbage perhaps? If so, the big guy would have been disappointed as the guard told me everything was pretty much emptied out at the time of his employment (early 1980's) but that the locals did dump lots of trash and refuse along the old dirt road that used to lead to the mix lot gates. Maybe the creature was feeding off this windfall and that was what drew him to the area? He also said he took pictures of the prints because he was amazed at the size but has long since lost them. He did add that although the prints looked just like a regular human's apart from their great size, the big toe on each foot was thicker and longer.

So, what ever became of the Cement Monster? Well, like many of his cryptid brothers he just faded out, moved on and was forgotten other than by the few that claimed to have seen or encountered him. I know some still say they find his prints from time to time in different areas of the wide valley, but no real eye-witness reports have come my way. Maybe he moved farther out into the desert and became known under a different moniker, like "The Yucca Man" or the "Hairy Brother", individuals we will encounter next in this chapter.

But now I'd like to move up the Death Valley, as even in that remote and searing environment we have reports and accounts of strange hairy man-beasts also being seen. Now if you've ever been to Death Valley, you know aside from the obvious flat and arid lowlands that give the place its name, there are also towering mountain ranges and lush highlands that support a wide range of plants and animals that one wouldn't regularly associate with a burning desert. The hot spots where the temperatures really soar are what one encounters while driving between and beneath these ranges, and it is mostly here that our hirsute "manimals" have been observed. Now the Native American tribes of the southwest maintain that these beasts live in the high peaks and ranges, but for a very credible reason modern humans seem to observe them mainly from the seat of a car as they dart across a remote road or trail – because that's how most people experience the desert these days – by just driving through. I have a good number of accounts featuring these types of things being seen crossing the roads in Death Valley, but as they lack any real detail and can get tedious after a while, I'll skip them in favor of more substantial sightings.

Today most of the people who venture into the high country are hardy backpackers, photographers and brush crews. But in the old days the heights were crawling with prospectors and miners as evidenced by the plethora of abandoned diggings and claims that dot the area. Here are a couple of stories from people who have been up in the ranges and report having encountered something strange.

The first story was told to me by a man I had met while working on another project a few years back, who had worked as a prospector for years in the area, as well as being a former Green Beret who served three tours of duty in Viet Nam. He was an expert tracker and was not someone who would be scared of things that go bump in the night. I asked him for permission to tell his story and he graciously agreed.

"A friend and I were camping up in the Panamints (*a short but spectacular range on the north side of the Mojave inside Death Valley National Park*) doing some exploring, looking for Indian artifacts, that kind of stuff. I'm thinking it was around 1973, because I was just back from my last tour. This was way back and you could still find all sorts of stuff left over from the old days, mining carts, pottery, colored glass bottles, all the stuff you can get a fortune for today – if you could still collect it.

Anyway, we had humped in about thirty miles and set up camp near an old mine that was set into a hillside just above a long sandy wash. The shaft had caved in so we couldn't go down it, we were just exploring the area around it as the miner's had left piles of junk and a few belongings behind. My friend Paul was really into collecting those old colored liquor bottles that they used in the late 1890's and the best place to find them was in the junk piles and heaps behind where the miners used to camp. We found a couple that were in pretty good shape, but mostly it was a bunch of broken junk that was rusty and razor sharp, and tons of rattlesnakes. I mean tons! The place was really "snaky" and since it was late summer and still furnace hot, you had to really watch your step at night if you got up to take a leak or walk around.

We had been there a couple of days and figured we

had pretty much scoured the place, and as our water was running out we decided to hump out the next day and maybe come back on another expedition later in the fall when it was a bit cooler and we could stay out longer. So that night we took it easy and just lounged around the fire smoking and talking, and it being a beautiful full moon night and our last one out, we decided we would walk up the sandy wash we were camped a few miles and just see what we found.

The wash led slightly uphill and then down through some pretty steep rock walls and as we walked I could see that there were some excellent gravel cuts exposed on them (*note - gold prospectors look for these "cuts" as they often are the remains of ancient stream beds and contain gold nuggets*) and so we kept going for about forty-five minutes thinking that maybe when we came back we would camp deeper up the wash and try our luck panning some of the gravels. Now were walking in the middle of the wash, on sand, leaving an obviously visible trail of our boot prints as we went, so finding our way back to camp wasn't going to be any problem, especially in the bright moonlight. After another half-hour, we decided to sit down on a rock ledge that jutted out like a perfect park bench, have a smoke and drink, then head back down the wash. And that's what we did.

But on our way back down the wash, we had maybe walked about twenty minutes when I saw something on our earlier tracks in the sand. Something had crossed our trail and left its own trail of footprints! Big bare human-like footprints that were at least eighteen inches long and half as wide! I could see it had come out from some rocks to our side, crossed our trail, where it stopped for a bit and turned around like it was looking about, then continued diagonally across the wash and up into the first rocky ledges of the opposite canyon wall. I could tell they were only minutes old and as our tracks were only forty-five minutes to an hour old at most, it must have just crossed our trail. We were standing there looking at them kind of in shock, when from up above us on the rock wall we heard some rocks clack and small stones falling. It sounded just like someone was walking along and slipped, or the footing was bad. Looking up into the darkness (that side of the canyon was in shadow from the moon) I couldn't see anything, but sensed that something was walking along the top of the canyon wall, almost parallel to us and in the same direction we were heading. Just being back from Nam I was still pretty combat cocky and quickly told Paul I had an idea. We would continue walking along the wash, talking in loud voices until we came to a bend or large boulder I could hide behind. He was to keep walking and talking out loud as if he was still conversing with me while I would lay back and see if I could see whatever was walking above us or maybe it would descend and try to follow him back to camp. The fact that who or whatever it was had feet eighteen inches long didn't really faze me, as I wasn't going to try and tackle it, I just wanted to try and get a look at it. And I had a .45 in my belt, so I knew if I had to I could defend myself.

So, when we came to a spot where the wash narrowed and there was a cluster of large boulders, I quickly slipped from his side and ducked behind the biggest one next to our trail. I could tell Paul was a little scared about going on by himself, but he did it without complaint, talking in a loud voice which I could hear pretty well until he had disappeared down the wash and around a bend leaving me in silence. I sat there absolutely still, like I was on ambush, just ears and eyes waiting for something to show itself. After about twenty minutes I again heard a bit of rock clack from the canyon wall above and figured whatever it was, it was on its way back down the wall and into the wash, and that I would then get a good look. But it didn't happen. I sat there for another half-hour or so, dead silent, but didn't hear or see a thing, so I decided my little plan hadn't worked and I would move out back down the wash to rejoin Paul at camp.

As soon as I stood up and stepped out from behind the boulder there was a huge crash and scrambling sound from the loose rocks up behind me a bit and then I could hear something tearing back up the sloped canyon wall and thought I just caught site of a large dark shape vaulting over the rim of the top rocks and out of view in a heartbeat. My hand was on my gun and my heart was beating like a rabbit! The thing had obviously been sitting up and behind me observing me all the time I was trying to get a look at him! Now the fact it had fled as soon as I stood up made me think it wasn't really dangerous, but the idea that something had reasoned out what I was up to, and then beaten me at my own game kind of sent an icy chill down my spine. You can bet I kept my hand on my gun as I backed out of the little cluster of boulders and quickly hoofed it down the wash back to our camp. The whole way I kept looking up, trying to make sure it wasn't above me and then I would quickly turn around to make sure it wasn't behind me until I was safely out of the little canyon and out onto the wash where it widened into a sort of plain. At that point too I could also see the glow of the fire Paul had started and stoked up for me, so I jogged down the wash and was soon sitting next to him by the fire drinking coffee and telling him what had happened. We both agreed that maybe one of us should stay awake on guard that night and then in the morning grab our finds and hump it out of there.

We each took two hour shifts, but nothing more happened, and with the sun coming up so early in the desert during the summer months, we were quickly packed and on our way. It was almost two years before we had the nerve to go back into that area, and although we have done many trips since then, we have never again seen or heard anything out of the ordinary."

If you've ever met or talked with a Green Beret, you know they are among some of the most highly educated and trained of our Special Forces soldiers, so I give his account some real credence. I asked him what he thought it might have been and he looked at me and said most sincerely - *Bigfoot, what else?* For him there was no doubt even though I did point out he hadn't actually seen the creature in question. Its prints and behavior was enough to convince him he was dealing with something quite extraordinary.

Now the next story I have is from a member of a road crew who was up on Hunter Mountain in Death Valley clearing brush from the road after a heavy storm, and *did* see something:

"This happened in about 2004, as I still have my map packet from the job. We were way back in the hills behind Hunter Springs cutting back some of the dead brush to make a sort of trail. At that time the park was looking to maybe make it a hiking spot and since we were already out there, we were ordered to try and make a better access. On the backside of the mountains it was pretty thick and it took us practically half the day just to hike in there with our saws and junk. I was on a crew with four other guys and we were supposed to climb up this ridge and begin falling some tangled junipers and then pile it in rows for the other crew with us to haul down the hill and pile in the open. I was the guy with the saw so I was leading my crew up onto the ridge. It was pretty steep and rocky, so I was taking my time threading my way through the brush, moving along this little rock outcropping to where I could begin cutting. The other guys behind me would then pull it out and toss the cut stuff down the hill and I would move to the next tree or tangle. I had just reached the end of the ridge and set my saw down to adjust my goggles, making a loud clang as the blade guard hit a rock, when I heard someone behind me yell "Hey, what the fuck's that?" Turning my head, I saw Ray, the oldest guy on the crew pointing off to his right yell, "It's a bear!" Then I heard someone else yell almost immediately, "No, it's not!" Turning to look, I just got a glimpse of something black and hairy tear through the brush just below me then crash off into the junipers. I never saw what it was, only that it was pretty damn big and moving like a freight train through the thorns and bushes. We could hear it crash down the brush on the other side of the ridge and then it was gone. I asked the kid who saw it best what it was, thinking we had scared up a black bear and he said "I don't know, but it had hands!"

"Hands?"

"Yeah, I saw its hands when it stood up. It grabbed a branch to pull itself up when you set the saw down. It must have been hiding down there."

He pointed to a spot in the tangle just under the lip of the ledge I was standing on.

"Man, it was big!"

"Sure it wasn't just a bear?"

"I don't know what it was but it had hands."

I looked at the other guys and they just shrugged, no one having seen it good enough other than the fact it was really big and hairy.

"The Hairy Man," Ray said and we all laughed at the kid that said he saw hands on it. So, thinking that was that, we started to work. I climbed down into the tangle under the ridge, got the saw going and started cutting away the thick trunks of the junipers. I had maybe been cutting for about ten minutes, with the other guys pulling the stuff out behind me when I cut through to what looked like a big nest or den area tucked up tight under the rocky ledge. It was about ten feet by ten feet and was all flattened down like something had been sleeping or laying up there. On some of the branches poking out there were tufts of long reddish black hair and the whole place had the smell of piss or wet dog. I shut the saw off and called the other guys to come have a look, thinking I had found a bear den and that was probably what we had scared out of there a little while earlier. They all crammed in and we were checking it out when Ray or someone went "Look at that!" We looked down to the ground where he was pointing and there were three of the biggest footprints I'd ever seen in the soft dirt right near the opening in the brush on the opposite side of the den. And I mean footprints! They looked just like a human's foot, five toes and all, but they were gigantic. No one had anything to measure them with, but I put my size 12 boot into one of them and there was at least five inches between the toe of my boot and the toe of the print. Massive!

We just kind of looked at each other and were like *holy shit*, what was that thing? Just then the radio crackled and the crew chief was asking why we weren't working and to quit fucking off. I guess he couldn't hear the saw or see us because we were all down under the ledge and figured we were goofing. Anyway, after that we went back to work but I know each of us was thinking about what if the thing came back, but nothing more happened. We just cleared out the whole area under the ledge, didn't find anything else other than a good-sized rattlesnake, and in about three hours we had the whole area cut back and cleared. Later in the afternoon on the way back to the trucks we talked about the thing, deciding that if there was such a thing as the Hairy Man, we'd probably seen one."

I don't want this particular chapter to be too big in this edition of Mojave Mysteries as I have copious accounts about these things, so I'm going to end by relating one last one from the beautiful Mojave National Preserve. It is three and half million acres of gorgeous wilderness that lays just between Death Valley and Joshua Tree National Park, bordering Nevada on its eastern side and framed by the two interstates. It details an experience with what the people down in the southern section of the California Mojave call "The Yucca Man", yet another hairy biped (or perhaps the same one) who haunts the sand and scrub.

Eddie C. is a hunter, a man who loves to spend his weekends out camped somewhere in the back of his truck or tent while stalking doves and rabbits. And although I don't hunt myself, I do respect his abilities in both tracking and observing animal behavior. Plus, he loves the solitude of remote places and is definitely not one to get spooked easily. In short, I find him to be completely believable and reliable. Which makes the following account all the more perplexing, because it is a weird one!

"I was hunting back in the mountains about seven miles north of the Fort Paiute ruins (*note – an old cavalry fort from the 1850's now a restored attraction*) near a hidden waterhole one of the old timers told me about. There's no other water sources for quite a bit around it and so is a hot spot for hunting. Everything goes there to drink. And around sundown it starts to get a heavy traffic of wildlife so I naturally hunt the slopes that lead up to it. I don't actually hunt near the waterhole, that would scare the animals off and I really only go to it a couple times a year so as not to disturb them too much. And I've never told anyone else its location either.

So, one fall about three years ago, this would be, oh, around 2011 or so, I was out there for a three-day trip hunting doves. I had been camping out of my truck and had a tent set up with a chair and stove on some rocks. I don't think I had a fire as there were regulations because of the drought.

Anyway, the first night I was sitting in my chair after having just arrived and having a cup of coffee. It was after sundown and just past twilight so it was pretty dark. I had a battery lantern going and was thinking of the next day's hunt when I heard something off to the right in the distance, upslope from me. There was a rising line of big boulders and the sound was coming from back of it. At least that's where I thought it was. It sounded like a gargling roar, not like a mountain lion's catty screams and much louder than any bobcat. If you've ever heard a bobcat up close, you know they can make a real strange low rasping growl that almost sounds like someone swearing. This was different. Really *LOUD* and if I had to put a picture to it, sounded like someone tearing a bear apart! I've never seen a bear in the Preserve and I'm sure they're there, but this was just massive sounding and it got my attention *really* quick. I stood up and listened and even walked over to my truck and got my gun out and loaded it. This kept up for maybe ten or fifteen minutes then just stopped cold. I listened closely, but couldn't hear any sounds like something coming down the slope or anything, so after another twenty minutes of not hearing it I figured I'd pack it in and go to sleep in my tent. I took the lantern into the tent with me. I also took my gun and also had my pistol with me, something I always sleep with when camping.

I was pretty beat from driving all day from San Diego,

so it didn't take long for me to fall asleep. I wasn't really feeling worried about the sound, more like curious. I've been a hunter long enough to know that inbred feeling when something is around, and certainly didn't have it that evening. In other words, whatever it was I didn't think it cared about me.

Until midnight.

I remember I was sleeping on my back with my arm over my chest when I snapped awake. Something woke me up with a start and it took a few seconds before I could recognize the mechanical sound I was hearing. Someone or something was messing with my truck! I could hear the springs creaking as whatever it was either rocked the thing or was standing on the bumper shaking it. Now I have a lift kit on my truck with some big springs, so to get it to rock that hard took some real effort or weight. I grabbed my pistol and sat up to listen more just as I heard something jump off the truck and land loudly in the gravel. It then began to walk around my camp site. I say "walk around" as I could distinctly hear steps. By now I was sure it was someone up to no good so I yelled out "Hey! Who's out there?!" which was pretty dumb because if they had a gun they could have just shot into the tent and got me. But I was still a little bleary so it came out before I really thought it through. The effect was instant. Whatever or whoever it was stopped dead and there was this instant dead silence. I had my pistol in my hand and listened. After about a minute or so, I thought it sounded like someone breathing really heavy, or taking short snorting breaths. It was pitch black out and without a fire I couldn't see anything outside the tent and there was no way I going to turn on the lantern and outline myself. I waited, sitting up in my sleeping bag and pointing my pistol in the direction I thought whatever was out there was standing. Then I heard a loud *chuff* or grunt and something ran by my tent and started

67

up the slope behind. I could hear their footsteps sounding clear as a bell on the gravel as they ran.

On two feet!

I listened as they just kept going for what I guessed was a few hundred yards until I couldn't hear them anymore.

It took me a few seconds to screw up the courage to open the tent, but I did and waited a few more moments before I jumped out with my pistol. I used the lantern and looked around but didn't see anything. I had left my flashlight in the truck so I had to go open the door to get it out before I could really look around. When I did I flashed it all over the area but didn't see anything. Looking around the truck I couldn't see any tracks as the ground was all stony, but where the "visitor" jumped off the back of the truck you could see two big marks in the gravel, not really any shape, just big dents in the soil where the gravel was stomped down. It took some weight, as my own boots hardly marked and I had been walking all over the camp site all evening. Nothing was missing or messed with on the truck, but I did notice the padlock on my lock box was now turned up instead of hanging down. That kind of bothered me because an animal wouldn't have the hands to mess with it and I wondered if there was now some desert kook or weirdo out there in the darkness. You know in the desert there are still hermits or solitary guys working illegal claims or meth labs and I didn't want to have to contend with that. I spent the rest of the night lying awake in my tent, but didn't hear anything else and by the time the sun was up I was able to get a bit of sleep.

I spent most the morning hanging around camp, wondering if I should just pack up and go to another spot, but since I couldn't find or see anything, by late afternoon I said "screw it" and went hunting. I guess I just figured it was some animal I had heard while half-asleep and since it hadn't bothered me, I wouldn't worry about it. Besides, I hadn't driven all that way not to do some hunting.

So around five o'clock I had made my way all along the ridges and up to the last line of big rocks before you get to the water hole. I had bagged a few doves and was just going to make one more sweep before I went back to camp, like I said, I don't like to get too close to the water so this was like my turn around point. I had just stepped into an open area where it was flat, with the water hole up the slope behind the last ridge to my right and the downslope to my left, like maybe a thirty-degree slope. Steep but not too bad.

Now as soon as I stepped into that spot I got the weirdest feeling. I literally could feel the hair on the back of my neck and arms stand up. I've hunted long enough to know that usually means something is around so I just stopped cold and listened. Nothing. Dead quiet. The feeling was so strong I actually unbuckled the flap on my holster as I only had birdshot in my shotgun and would have to use my .357 if anything came at me. But like I said, I hadn't heard or seen anything, just felt it.

Suddenly, out of the corner of my eye I saw something come flying out of the bushes near the ridge to my right. It was big and "wind milling" through the air as it arced out and down toward where I was standing. I couldn't tell what the hell it was other than it being large and gray. It landed in a bunch of bushes near me with a good *thump* and shower of dirt. This was really bizarre. I took a step over to the bushes and saw it was a goddamn burro! Like a young burro, laying on the ground on its side, dead! Its eyes were open, but it was bent like backwards in a U-shape! Its backbone snapped. I'm telling you, I was like "*what the fu-* ", when I heard that loud roar again, but this time *REALLY* close! I wheeled around and just for a second I saw something really big and brown duck down from between two rocks up in the same direction the flying donkey came from. I couldn't really tell what it was, but it had hair, brown hair and looked like the upper part of a person. I only saw it from the bottom of the chest up, but I definitely saw a head on some huge shoulders and one arm when it ducked down.

That was it for me!

I felt so strange, like drunk or something with the fear. I just backed up and kept my eyes on those rocks in case the thing charged me but I never saw it again. I listened hard, but couldn't hear any steps or noises, so I couldn't tell if it had run off or was still up there, I just knew I going to get the f--k out of there!

I didn't even look at the dead burro again, I just backed down the ridge for a ways (sic) and then turned around and hurried down to where my camp was. It was so damn strange I just couldn't wrap my head around it. I just broke camp in a hurry and decided to cut short my trip and go home. Didn't tell my wife or anything, just said the hunting sucked and the weather was bad. I've only told a few people because it's just so damn weird and crazy. But I've had time to think about it and can tell you this – I looked at the ridge the donkey came flying off of and there was no way it could have just fallen and landed near me. I distinctly saw it arc up and over the rocks before crashing down next to me. Something *threw* it at me! And smashed its back too. It was folded up pretty good. And the strength to do that and throw it in the air for like fifty yards? Forget about it, it would take a superman. And the hairy thing in the rocks? I got no clue, but it was there and I heard it as well as saw it. I used to think people that saw shit like Bigfoot and that kind of stuff were just plain nutzo, but now – and in the desert? I never heard about the "Yucca Man" till you told me about it, but I guess I'm one of the nuts now too."

I hardly think Eddie is a "nut", but the flying donkey part of the story always makes me shake my head. Talk about the "high weirdness" factor! And believe me, I grilled him good about it and he swore up and down it happened as he related it above, right down to acting out how the thing flew through the air and landed beside him. I can only wonder why the Yucca Man felt compelled to kill an innocent burro just to scare someone off instead of jumping out or simply throwing a rock, but who knows? Maybe the big guy knows what a gun is and how quick humans are to use one? Either way, it makes for an excellent Mojave Mystery and deliciously satisfyingly bizarre conclusion to this volume's chapter on the hairy "man beasts" of the desert.

Ghosts, Orbs, Giants and Underground Cities

When I was growing up, there always seemed to be several types of ghost stories going around. The most popular usually centered on someone driving in the middle of nowhere who picked up a lone hitchhiker, invariably pale and thin, who would afterwards prove to have been a ghost. A common theme was that they had been the victim of a murder or horrible accident and now haunted the stretch of road where it happened. A typical one went like this; a man was driving through the countryside one night when he stopped and picked up a young woman who was out by herself on the roadside. She was silent, wouldn't say much and just sat beside him watching the road ahead. He drives along for a bit trying to engage her in conversation but finally gives up and just motors on. Then it happens – he turns to say something and she's gone, or she's turned into some hideous ghoul/skeleton/demon, or she now gives him some piece of advice and then opens the door and dives out never to be seen again. And of course, when the scared motorist arrives at the next diner/gas station/truck stop he is informed that he's just seen "the ghost of that young woman killed years ago on the same road, etc.". It was a format used often in our tales and we all just knew it had to be true no matter how many times we heard the same set up. And when I got older and started studying stuff like this, I found that they had a historical precedent. Many tales were told in the 1800's of "phantom brakemen" or "ghostly coach drivers" who warned people traveling by wagon or buggy of a dangerous river crossing ahead, or signaled train engineers that the bridge just down the tracks was washed out or destroyed. And yes, all too proved to have been victims of earlier catastrophes at the designated locations who now sought to warn their still living brethren.

Now in the Mojave, we also have our own version of this type of repeating ghostly intervention, but it doesn't usually involve roads or transport, it almost always is centered around haunted mines. In the desert, there are literally thousands of old and abandoned mines and many have stories of ghosts or spirits that haunt them. And why not? The vast and lonely desert was and still is a mecca for people seeking mineral riches and many have perished, often quite violently through accident, ill fortune or outright criminal treachery in their attempt to gain fabulous wealth. I could fill a bible-sized book with stories of haunted mines, but as they all pretty much seem to follow the same formula as the hitchhiking ghost stories I described above, I'm going to limit this edition of Mojave Mysteries to just a few good mine hauntings I have uncovered.

The first one involves a young worker who was killed at the Virginia Dale Mine down in the appropriately named Dale Mining District near Twentynine Palms, California. The area was a booming mining hub in the late 1800's until the early 1900's when it was pretty much abandoned and fell silent. Many mines and shafts still exist among the rugged hills drawing hundreds of desert rats and explorers every year who enjoy wandering the rugged area and looking at the old diggings and ruins. Now to say Virginia Dale Mine is to give the impression of one great tunnel in the earth with men working like ants around the clock to pry the precious ore from the rocky soil, but that would be a mistake. Often it was a series of small shafts or excavations that were claimed and worked by a company of miners, being grouped together under a single name for ease and legal registering purposes. And so, our paranormal tale didn't begin at the Virginia Dale proper, but at one of the smaller shafts, the Oak Mine in the claimed location. On February 21st, 1900, *The Los Angeles Herald* carried a small article stating that a certain "Riley

Myers" was killed in a cave in when the tunnel he was shoring up collapsed and crushed him. He was working alone and when found the unfortunate guy was discovered pinned against a wall by tons of rock with his head and upper torso horribly mangled. The body being retrieved by his poor wife and brother; the young miner was then laid to rest miles away from the scene of the accident back near Los Angeles.

Now I should say that most of the mines down in the Dale District have been sold and resold over the years and finding the exact location of many is difficult because they have been renamed by their subsequent owners so often one mine will have several titles. The Virginia Dale Mine site proper is still identifiable, but the exact shaft that was deemed the Oak Mine is still debatable. Why does this matter? Because I like to visit as many of these places as I can, and I have not been able to determine the exact location of this shaft. My sources for this tale are several of the off-roaders and motocross bikers that like to use the area on the weekends, and it is from them that the story of the ghost of Riley Myers comes.

Jason L. is an avid off-roader and amateur paranormal investigator. His passion is EVP or "Electronic Voice Phenomenon" as it's styled by proponents. To avoid a lengthy explanation, suffice it to say it involves using sound recording equipment to obtain evidence of ghostly voices or sounds in supposedly haunted spots. I know some people swear they can also record angels, demons and other ecto-spirits, using complex and highly sensitive gear, but for this story we will deal with his simple process of leaving a small battery sound recorder in a spot to try and pick up any weird or strange sound. At least that's how Jason and his friends like to do it.

The story had been going around in his riding group that some of them had encountered a ghostly figure near the

Virginia Dale Mine, usually late at night and then only fleetingly. They said it looked like a guy in old work clothes, with his head and upper body soaked in blood and one arm dangling by his side – almost the exact injuries reported to have happened to poor Riley Myers back in 1900. He would be seen standing at the entrance to one of the open shafts or nearby, and upon being sighted would turn and instantly flee into the one of the open tunnels and disappear. Some said they had stopped to see if it was someone who truly needed assistance, but could never find him or coax anyone to answer from deep in the shafts. It was a bit of local folklore and no one really took the story seriously until Jason decided to do some EVP recording down in a couple of the shafts and came back with something very interesting. Camping nearby one night in December of 2008, he and a girlfriend powered up their small Sony recorder and placed it deep within one of the smaller shafts, just at the place where the tunnel ended due to falling rock and shattered timbers. Leaving it on a bit of discarded lumber, they turned it to record and then retreated to their campsite for the night. In the morning, they retrieved the device and after a day of riding and having fun in the Dale District, they went home to listen to the recording at length. Jason said he first gave it a quick check at the site with some cheap ear buds, but as the recording was almost four hours in length he didn't really get a good chance to examine it until back home. There he would put it on while playing his Gameboy or just working on his motorcycle. I'll let him tell the good part:

"I had been listening for like an hour or so, and it was mostly just silent or maybe the distant sound of wind blowing across one of the vents or openings, pretty common with most mine recordings. Then I heard what sounded like a grumble or croak, like someone imitating a bull frog, you know? That's the best I can describe it. A low grunt. Then it got a little louder and sounded like whatever it was came right up to the recorder. There was a little bit of static too sometimes. A one point whatever it was moved or bumped the recorder because it thumped and made a plastic sound. Then for about thirty seconds it sounded like someone talking or mumbling, real low and deep down in their chest."

Now I should add that often people who like to practice this stuff say you have to slow the recording way down to hear some of the alleged sounds and voices, and sometimes ever reverse the sound to make sense of it. That's what Jason did on his computer after hearing the weird noises. He continued:

"I had it on the scope so I could see the exact sounds I wanted to slow and play. My software lets me do it super easy. At just the point where the thing sounds closest to the Sony I distinctly heard it say the same thing three times. You have to listen really close, 'cuz when I turn up the level the hiss comes up way loud too, but I swear you can hear a voice say "*Help*", "*Help Me*" or maybe "*Help It*". It's there! And in a man's voice, a deep man's voice. Everyone I've played it for gets real quiet when they hear it. F—king spooky."

Okay, I bet your first question is "have you heard it?". Yes, I have. But I have to admit although I could definitely hear something on the recording, I'm not sure I could make out the words Jason swears are there. To my ears it sounds like some deep grumble or exhalation repeated several times and since you can definitely hear something bump the recorder, I can't help wondering if it might not be some curious animal or bird in the mine checking out something new in its nocturnal environment. Anyone who has spent any time around old mines can tell you that often times various animals will make use of a cool shaft to stay out of the searing desert sun or bring its food back to in order to eat in peace and security. And not to mention the millions of bats that roost in these old mines and shafts skittering to and fro all night long. But as to the story of Riley Myers, all I can say is that the repeated sighting of the spectral figure with wounds matching his, along with it being in the exact historical location of his demise and the plea for help does make it a mystery worth relating.

One thing I wonder about though, is the article in the 1900 paper says he was crushed badly and killed instantly by the falling of many tons of rock, so there would have been no time for him to utter a cry for help. And the body was removed by relatives and buried elsewhere – so why would his ghost hang around such a remote and forlorn place now and still plead for assistance? Perhaps it seeks solace from dying in such a lonely fashion or, and I hope this isn't the case, it seeks to draw some unsuspecting soul to their doom farther in the aged digging, where the timbers are now completely dried and rotten and the tons of rock above loose and unsteady? Something to bear in mind next time you feel the urge to enter one of these dangerous abandoned shafts.

Our next haunted mine story takes place many miles to the north of the Dale Mining District, up in the Mojave National Preserve and just past the old "town" of Cima. I am including it because I visited it personally twice in preparation for writing this book and got to explore the "haunted" cabin and outbuildings. Strangely enough, it's named the "Death Valley Mine" despite the fact it *isn't* even in Death Valley! A fairly well-preserved collection of buildings, old equipment and poorly-fenced shafts, it was established in 1906, when the mine sporadically produced gold until the 1930's. It was pretty much abandoned before being reopened for a while in 1950's and most of the present rusty ruined equipment lying about dates from that time. Caretakers lived on the property from the 50's through the 70's and it is from them that the tales of hauntings and paranormal activity come. The main building still standing looks like it might have been an office as it is much larger than some of the smaller cabins dotting the site, and for some reason seems to attract the bulk of the ghostly visitations. Perhaps the ghosts of the former miners still come seeking the pay and compensation they still feel they are entitled to? Lord knows they would have earned it working out in that heat and the dangerous conditions that anyone would have encountered underground. In fact, caretakers in the 1970's who ventured down into one of the collapsed shafts found the remains of hundreds of birds and small animals who had crawled down seeking relief from the oppressive heat and drawn to the moisture below before finding themselves trapped with no way to crawl back out. Their numerous skeletons litter the ground to this day and are certainly joined by many more unfortunates since that time.

But what kind of haunting or visitations were recorded at this site? I have two reports to relate. The first is from an elderly gentleman who worked as a caretaker back in the late 1950's and swore even then the main building, still somewhat in use, was haunted. I got his story second hand from a friend and really the only details I heard were that the place "had ghosts and was haunted" with the large building being where most of the action took place. Not much to go on, but I share it to show that even people that lived on site early on believed there was paranormal activity present. The second account I have is much more detailed – and tantalizingly strange.

Mark D. is a photographer from Milwaukee who specializes in picture essays of travels around the American Southwest. On a trip where he was featuring old post offices in remote places, he happened to be up in the Mojave NP doing a shoot at the old post office in Cima, now a "ghost town" itself, although calling it a "town" is extremely generous. It's more like a few buildings crumbling away and some rusty junk heaped alongside the railroad line. Since my very first trip through the area some fifteen years ago a few of the standing buildings have now collapsed into nothing more than piles of rotting boards full of rusty nails – and lots of snakes, so be careful if you go poking around. Anyway, he was visiting Cima when he heard of the old Death Valley Mine and decided to head up there and check it out.

"I was going to shoot some of the old cabins at magic hour (*note – sundown when the sunlight is very evocative*) and then head on up to Vegas for the night. When I got to the mine, there was so much cool stuff to see and shoot I ended up pretty much occupied until it was dark. I ended up using a flash to get some great shots of the screech owls that inhabited the place. They'd sit there staring down at me from the old rafters in some of the decayed buildings and I got some pretty amazing close ups.

I was coming out of the last little cabin at the edge of the place, looking up past the main building toward where I had parked my car. It was dark enough that I had to wait a few minutes for my eyes to adjust to the night after using my flash. While standing there, I thought I saw a flashlight or light being turned on in the big building, except it looked rather purplish, not like a regular white light. For a second I thought someone else was maybe out there too, but when I looked where my car was parked I couldn't see any other vehicles. I knew there was no power to the place, I had been in that building earlier and aside from a really dodgy floor (it was rotten and I feared falling through) there wasn't much in it aside from some old cabinets and empty shelves. So I knew it couldn't be a night light or security light coming on. Besides, the place was completely abandoned or at least looked it. I didn't even see any footprints in the dirt along some of the lanes that lead to the empty cabins earlier when I was walking around.

Going up toward the building on my way to my car, I looked at the open doorway as I passed by and instantly froze. There was something or someone sitting on the porch of the big building! At first I thought it was a person being perfectly still and watching me but then it got up and moved along the railing on four feet and I could see it looked like either a big black dog or a wolf. There aren't any wolves I know of up there, but the thing was way bigger than a coyote and the only thing I could think of was a dog. Now you might think so what, a dog, right? But you should know that roaming packs of wild or feral dogs out in the west have been responsible for some pretty nasty attacks resulting in people and pets getting badly mauled. So I stood real still and watched it silently lope off around the corner of the building and disappear from sight. Not seeing it again I kept going to my car and after throwing my bag and gear in the back, jumped in and got ready to leave.

Except the car wouldn't start.

A brand-new rental and it's like totally dead. Wouldn't even turn over, just *click* – *click* – *click*.

Shit!

I'm no mechanic, and I didn't have cell service so I just decided to spend the night in the car and then walk down the road a few miles in the morning and try to call someone. I had a few bars signal when I was making the trip up from Cima, so I figured I'd be able to get some help. I make sure to always carry a list of all local garages or ranger stations in the areas I visit so I'm not ever totally stranded. And I'd spent plenty of nights in a car while doing these shoots, so putting the seat back and trying to get some sleep was not that big a deal either. Not too comfortable, but doable. I also figured I could at least get some sun up shots too which might make for a better article.

So that's what I did, got in and more dozed off and on than slept for a couple of hours. I had the window cracked a bit on the passenger side as it was still pretty warm out, and was laid back at about a forty-five-degree angle when I heard something. Or thought I heard something. I was kind of in a half-sleep and had my eyes closed when I again heard something growl or grunt near the opposite door. Opening my eyes and looking over, I didn't see anything until I turned my head back and looked straight ahead.

There was that big black dog thing again, standing in the middle of the path that lead from the parking area to the mine buildings!

It was dark but I could see its outline against the lighter ground. It was just sort of standing there looking straight at me, or at least right at the front of the car like it knew I was sitting there staring back. I was just about to try and turn on the headlights to see it better when suddenly from the large main building off behind it there was another quick purplish flash of light like I'd seen earlier. Like someone turning the lights on and off super quick. Instantly the big dog turned and looked at the building. There was another flash and then the dog ran straight to the building and bounded up the steps. It was like someone was calling the dog back, but I didn't see or hear anything. Just a couple of flashes of light. I wasn't too scared at first when I saw the dog again as I felt rather safe locked in the car, but seeing the light I suddenly thought there *might* be someone in the old building and what if they had a gun or something? Then I got pretty scared. Sitting in the car I felt trapped, if someone came out I didn't know what I was going to do. I waited and watched but thank God didn't see anything else all the rest of the night. I didn't get much sleep obviously and when dawn came I contemplated getting out and walking back down the long road to try and make a call. But I was now worried if that dog was still out there it might come after me so it was a little bit until I had the guts to open the door and get out. I also had to take a leak pretty bad. I was just about to open the door when for some reason I decided to turn the key again and see what happened.

The engine started right up!

I mean I had tried and tried all evening before and nothing, but now it started no problem! I can't tell you how flipping happy I was about that – but I did still have to piss so I left the engine running and opened the door and got out. I did the deed all the while keeping an eye on the big building in case you know who came out. But no dog. With the door open and engine running I decided to walk a few yards to the start of the trail where I'd seen the thing standing looking at me and see if there were any tracks.

Nothing.

In the dust I could clearly see my boot tracks but no dog tracks. Okay, then. This was getting too weird. I decided *to hell* with the morning shots, I wasn't going to risk turning the engine off again and possibly running into the dog, so I got back in the car and drove off. I got back down to Cima and after a quick stop headed out to the highway. Part of me has always wished that I'd gone over to the old office building and looked inside to see what could have made those purple light flashes, but the other part of me knows that would have been really stupid, especially if that was a huge wild dog hanging around the place. After you told me about other people seeing things out there I wondered if I might have encountered something paranormal, but I've never heard of a ghost having a dog, but who knows? It was definitely weird."

I can't say what Mark might have seen, but I do know in ghost lore there is the story of the black dog, a huge hound that sometimes haunts an area or whose sighting is a harbinger of death. But do they have ghostly masters as his story implies? I'm not sure, but I'm glad to report last time I heard from him, Mark was still in good health and staying busy.

Now there is something to the purple flashes he saw, and I can relate that I've heard of the phenomena being reported many times over, especially in connection with old mines and cabins. Many people have recorded seeing "orbs", small floating balls of light or energy in these remote and lonely places, which usually appeared after sundown and often at times seemed to react or interact with the person observing them. Some have reported feeling the presence of something dark or malevolent when encountering them, while others have expressed just the opposite – the orbs seemed alive and almost playful, like fireflies on a nightly romp. Spirits of the dead? Other life forms? Or as some physicists' have postulated; spontaneous bursts of electromagnetic energy or plasma generated by geological pressures deep underground due to plate tectonics? I can't say, but my files are full of reports, and in the interest of brevity I will only offer one more in this particular volume of Mojave Mysteries, and as I have visited the place myself, can give a better description of the scene.

Up in Death Valley National Park, just past "The Racetrack", a flat area famous for its mysterious moving rocks (just recently explained as being caused by the wind moving rocks on the super slick mud when the odd rain hits), if one travels down a long dirt trail named Lost Burro Mine road you will come to, with no surprise – the Lost Burro Mine. A fantastic old mining camp that offers the hardy visitor an awesome collection of buildings, numerous shafts, tons of rusting equipment and a huge mill that is still standing. A photographer's dream, the place is set on the slopes of a richly-colored mountain that just screams mineral wealth. The story of the mine's founding is equally colorful. In 1907 the tale goes, a man chasing after an escaped pack burro decided he'd had enough of running through the boulders and heat following the ornery beast and to give vent to his pent-up anger reached down and picked up a rock to throw at the braying escapee. Noticing the rock seemed rather heavy for its size, and being a prospector, he broke it open and found it contained a rather sizable assortment of gold nuggets. Eureka! Soon a sizable operation was humming away on the spot which promised vast riches for all involved, but as with many of these outfits, various problems and calamities plagued the various companies that tried to capitalize on the venture. Gold was brought out, but after a bountiful run of several decades the mine fell silent and was eventually abandoned. Today it's a favorite spot for 4x4 enthusiasts and off-road adventurers. And it's from these dusty visitors that I have gathered several reports of orbs.

Seen mainly around the main cabin, but also witnessed near the openings of some of the large timbered shafts that bore into the mountain side like giant termite tunnels, they have been unanimously reported as being seen manifesting themselves like small glowing soap bubbles floating on the breeze.

Even when there is *no* breeze.

Apparently able to propel themselves around, the orbs are seen circling about objects or darting in and out of the cabin windows. Most people say that they vanish when approached and do so silently as a group. The accounts are pretty uniform;

"I was walking up to the cabin and looking about when I heard my daughter say *hey, look!* She was pointing to the left side of the cabin and I saw what looked like little puff balls of light circling around and going in the window. They looked like flies or bees, but were just little sparkly lights. We ran up to the cabin but when we went inside there was nothing to be seen. No lights. We never saw anything after that. My son said it was probably just dust hanging in the air with the setting sun behind it, but I saw them too. They were definitely balls of light."

And another report of the Lost Burro orbs:

"Was by the old outhouse taking pictures and turned around to say something to my buddy. Looked past him by the cabin and there was (sic) these light balls drifting in and out of the front door. Kind of spooky. But cool. We tried to take pictures but the minute we went over there they went out."

Pretty standard sightings, if such a thing can be said of something arguably supernatural or at least at present scientifically undocumented. No feelings of dread or malice, just simple observances. Now this next one is a little more detailed. It happened to several people that went back deep into one of the open tunnels. Now I don't recommend anyone do this as the timbers that shore up the roof and sides of these diggings are dry and rotten and it wouldn't take much to bring several hundred tons of rock down upon your head should you be unlucky enough to be in there during one of California's frequent earth tremors. And in some spots even brushing against some of the beams might do the trick as they are under a terrific amount of pressure. But some people still risk it (I have to admit we desert explorers have all done it at times, but please recognize it's pretty stupid and good way to get into trouble) and have lived to tell the tale.

"A couple of friends and I were up at the Lost Burro. We were checking out some of the adits (*note – a horizontal shaft opening*) and followed one at the top of the ravine back several under yards. It came to a spot where there was a vertical shaft but the roof had collapsed for the most part, blocking the way any farther. I was on all fours looking under some of the fallen beams when I saw a bunch of little light ball things floating around behind the rock fall. I called my friends over and we watched them for a few minutes trying to figure out what the hell they were. It's pitch black in there and when we killed our flashlights you couldn't see your hand in front of your face if you tried. But the lights you could see, slowly circling around each other and then winking out now and then. They were about the size of those little Christmas lights. We tried to get some video with our phones but the second we tried they vanished! Gone. After sitting there for about twenty minutes and videoing we crawled back out. Never saw them again anywhere else.

None of us had ever heard of orbs before, so it was pretty cool seeing them."

Is the Lost Burro haunted? I don't know as I can't find any reports of accidents or murders at the mine, but as an interesting footnote to the accounts above, I did find this old article when doing some research. It's from the August 23rd, 1907 edition of *The Sacramento Union*, which would put it right at the beginning of the mine's operations.

DIED ON THE EDGE OF DEATH VALLEY

GOLDFIELD (Nev.), Aug. 22. —Tom Cornish, one of the best-known mining engineers in the country and formerly superintendent of the Stratton Independence mine at Cripple Creek, died at the Stenikas ranch on the edge of Death Valley yesterday of pneumonia. Mr. Cornish started for the Funeral range of mountains several days ago in company with a party of Eastern capitalists for an inspection of the Lost Burro group of claims. When near the Stenikas ranch Cornish, who was a sick man when he left Goldfield, became so ill that his companions were compelled to leave him at the ranch while they returned to this city and sent a physician to attend him. News of Mr. Cornish's death was received in Goldfield today and an automobile was at once sent to the ranch to bring in the body.

Maybe the soul or restless energy of poor Tom Cornish made its way to the shafts of the Lost Burro to complete his ghostly inspection and is somehow connected to the reports of orbs being seen there? A reach perhaps, but possibly a suitable candidate for a spectral visitation don't you think?

Unfortunately, like so many of these puzzling paranormal and extraordinary manifestations, the orbs seen by many seem to vanish whenever a camera comes out. A sentient decision or proof of fabrication? Again, not having witnessed the phenomenon myself I'll withhold judgement but I'd sure like to see some pictures or good video because it sounds fascinating. The only pictures I've ever seen offered for the existence of orbs has come from some researchers in Russia and I can't vouch for their authenticity. Now I have read about scientists postulating that the grinding of the tectonic plates deep underground, especially granite formations, can cause a sudden discharge of static electricity that can be viewed on the surface terrain as a spark or sudden flash of light. It's called a piezoelectric effect and many crystals (which granite is full of) can have these properties. In areas prone to seismic activity, these flashes have been given the name "earthquake lights" and are said to happen immediately before or during an earthquake. Could this somehow be an explanation for or even a possible generator of orbs? Many people living the Mojave have reported seeing strange lights and flashes on numerous occasions and many of these localities lie near or along known fault lines. A quick perusal of older newspapers will turn up many articles such as this one from *The Desert Sun* from October 30th, 1974:

MYSTERY LIGHT

A large flash of light around 9 p.m. Tuesday touched off a flood of phone calls to local law enforcement agencies. The Desert Sun made a check of various agencies to determine the origin of the light, but was unable to locate the source. Southern California Edison Company spokesman said they had a transmission line relay kickout around 10:05 p.m. but did not think it was the cause of the sighting.

Go back almost thirty years earlier and we find more evidence of strange lights and flashes. This again from *The Desert Sun* of June 22nd, 1948.

MYSTERY LIGHTS POLICE UNABLE TO TRACK SOURCE OF FLASHES

Police Friday night investigated reports of mysterious lights flashing from the mountainside in the southwestern section of the Village but were unable to find any trace. The report was made to police by Councilwoman Ruth Hardy of the Ingleside Inn who reported seeing a light being flashed on the mountainside as if someone were signaling. Officer Robert White investigated but reported back that he was unable to see the lights and that if anyone were signaling from the mountain side they had stopped before the location could be determined.

Now looking back even farther, I found this article that describes almost the same occurrences as reported by the explorers at the Lost Burro Mine in Death Valley. It comes from *The Los Angele Herald*, May 6th, 1881:

AN ENCHANTED CAVE

A party of New Mexican miners, while prospecting near Mesilla, on a spur of the mountains recently discovered a passage which led into the rock at a downward angle of about 45 degrees. Impelled by curiosity, three of the party, steadied by a lariat field by the others, started down the tunnel, under the mountain. The passage was rough and uneven, and about four feet high. By the light of a candle they found 20 feet farther a large hall completely filled with long, delicate columns, reaching from the floor upward out of sight. They were stalactites, hanging from the walls in endless variety, while from the floor rose rich stalagmites, meeting them and forming figures of all conceivable shapes. Unfortunately, the candle was extinguished and nothing could be done but follow the lariat back. As their eyes became accustomed to the gloom a curious phenomenon appeared, in various parts of the cave luminous spots of light were seen. Some near them gave out fitful flashes of flame, while ethers seemed like moons, glowing with a pale-yellow light; others again were of irregular shape, that made the darkness more apparent. Every move revealed new wonders. Oval balls of light blazed from behind the columns, confronting them at every step, while as far as they could see, gleaming and sparkling, the mysterious lights appeared, making the cavers a realization of the old tales of enchantment.

I also have a longer tale of orbs from the desert from around the same time, but this one contains elements of ghostly precognition and a decidedly more lethal outcome. It comes from the December 2nd, 1894 edition of *The San Francisco Call*:

"WE SAW A ROUND, STRANGE COLORED LIGHT"

A Mystery of the Desert

Colonel Whitehead is a story-teller from way back and has a reputation as a raconteur that spreads over a dozen Western States and Territories, and from the waters of the Atlantic to those of the Pacific. He has had innumerable thrilling adventures, both in war and in peace, and when in the proper humor he will spin yarns of the most absorbing interest by the hour. One story that he related as we were jogging along behind the mules on a recent trip to the undoubted gateway of sheol (sic) (i. c., the sulfur banks of Kern County) is so uncanny and strange that I will venture to repeat it.

Some three years ago, said the Colonel, I was engaged in making a survey from Rogers, on the Mojave Desert, to Antioch. We had made rapid progress toward Fort Tejon Pass, and it became necessary to check up the line, measuring distances from Government corners, that the road might be accurately located upon the filing map. This work was assigned to an odd genius whom I will call "Buck," a man past 65, tough as a knot and as wicked as a pirate. Frequently be would set his rickety old transit with the lens wrong end to, and after trying to locate the flag for fifteen or twenty minutes he would discover his error and then such swearing as he indulged in is rarely heard outside the forecastle of a man-of-war. I sometimes think the strange manifestation which I am about to relate to you might have been due to Buck's profanity. Certainly, if man can have power to summon spirits, evil or good, from the nether world Buck ought to have had that power in no small measure.

I began the inspection of the survey preparatory to the right-of-way work, starting at Rogers, a desolate station on the A. and P. road, on the borders of an immense dry lake. We made our first camp Borne fifteen miles west of that point. The regular survey camp was at this time near Gorman's station, under the shadows of Mount Frazier. Our camp was a rude settler's cabin, and near it was a shack barn with a little hay stored in it. A well of fairly good water close by made a comfortable camp a possibility. It was late in October, and the water had risen near the surface in the bed of the dry lake. We had eaten our supper the first night out, and were having a quiet smoke, looking out over the desolate expanse of desert toward Lancaster, a station on the Southern Pacific road some twenty-five or thirty miles to the southwest. Buck had been entertaining us with yarns about ghosts that he insisted haunted an old mining camp near Owens Lake, and was inclined to feel hurt because I laughed at his tales.

When darkness came on and only the outlines of the gaunt mountains across the desert were discernible in the starlight. Buck of a sudden said, "Colonel, I never thought an engine headlight could be seen so plainly at Lancaster."

"Nor did I," was my reply, as I saw close to the ground at a distance difficult to estimate a round, strange-colored light or ball of fire, very like a locomotive headlight. A moment's watching, however, soon convinced me that the light was erratic in its movements and was nothing more or less than a grand display of the "ignis fatuus" or will o' the wisp, something I had seen many times at the ends of the spars or mastheads of a ship at sea, but never on land or in such magnitude. I said to Buck: "It's no headlight. It's one of your ghosts come to convince me of the truth of your stories." He turned white as a sheet and grasped me by the arm, saying, "It's coming dead for us, sure as we live."

And so it was; dancing up and down It came nearer and nearer. I must confess it made even me a trifle nervous, while as for Buck be evidently took my joke about the ghosts in dead earnest and was completely panic-stricken. "For God's sake!" he cried. "Let us get out of this," and was on the point of jumping up and running off into the desert, when all of a sudden the light disappeared and was seen no more that night.

Buck finally quieted down, though I could see by his nervousness and frequent quick glances in the direction in which the light bad appeared that he was still in dread of its reappearance.

I discussed the matter with him for hours, trying to explain the real nature of the phenomenon and that no possible harm could come of it. But he would not have it that way, and all that I could say did not influence his superstitious dread of the strange appearance.

"Colonel," he said, "it's a hoodoo. This railroad scheme and its promoters will die suddenly. Surely."

I laughed at his fears and we laid down to rather a restless night. The work in this section was not completed next day in time to return to the main camp, and a dozen times in the course of the work Buck spoke about the "ghosts," as he persisted in calling the phenomenon, and he was even more muddied than usual in his manipulation of the transit. Finally, his slowness caused night to come on before our task was completed, and we therefore returned at dusk to the same camping place as the night before.

After we had eaten supper Buck said:

"Colonel, I never want to see that Infernal light again. Ghosts or no ghosts, it's no good and no luck will come of it." The words were scarcely cut of his mouth when, apparently not more than a hundred yards away, the huge ball of fire appeared like a flash, dancing up and down and seemingly coming dead toward us. Now Buck became almost beside himself with terror." Let's go, and the quicker the better," shouted my now thoroughly alarmed companion; but suddenly, as on the previous night, the light vanished. Buck then recovered some portion of his equanimity, and though he was still anxious to return to camp I finally persuaded him that there was danger that we would lose our way if we ventured out on the desert; after dark, while if we remained there was nothing to be afraid of. Neither of us slept much, however, for I must confess that I had a sort of "creepy" sensation myself, and we were up early next morning, completed our work and got an early start back to camp. While we were on the road Buck said: "Colonel, I don't want to discourage you, but the people who are at the head of this scheme to build a competing railroad will die suddenly and this work will stop. In fact, I wouldn't wonder if you and I both went over the range with them to keep them company. But they are going, sure!" "How will you know," I replied, and I could say no more, as my backers were then unknown.

Now let me tell you the strange sequel. The very same week that Buck made his prediction the Barings failed. Early in November Henry D. Minot, the leading spirit and financial head of the enterprise, was killed in a railroad accident while returning from Washington, D. C, where he had concluded the purchase of General Beale's ranches in every detail, save the passing of the parsers and paying the money, the intention having been to subdivide that immense estate of 264,000 acres.

On Thanksgiving Day of the same month came orders to close the work, discharge everybody, and break camp. The following year Allan Manvel, president of the Atchison, Topeka and Santa Fe road, died after a brief illness, he having been the second backer of this great enterprise, and. soon followed the death of Mr. Magoun of the great banking-house of Baring, Magoun & Co., the third and last of the promoters of a rival railroad to the Southern Pacific system."

"What became of Buck?" I asked as the colonel

paused.

"Buck? Just read that clipping," and the colonel took from his pocket-book a worn bit of newspaper and handed it to me. It read as follows

Bagdad, Colorado Desert, January 16, 1889. -A gold prospector and surveyor known as "Buck" Pomeroy disappeared mysteriously from his camp at this place three days ago and no trace of him has been found. He was in company with two friends, and was apparently in good health and spirits. They all retired as customary early in the evening but in the morning Buck was missing, and diligent search has failed to find him. He went away just as he was rolled in his blankets— barefooted and half-dressed. One of his men said he thought be heard Buck's voice in the night saying something about some ghosts being after him, but be thought it was a dream and so paid no attention to it. Buck has evidently joined that innumerable caravan of men whose bones whiten the remote sections of the desert, and will doubtless remain forever without burial.

I folded up the clipping and returned it to the colonel. He put it back in his pocket-book without a word.

G. F. W.

I must admit it's beyond my scope as an author, but I have at times often thought people truly might be witnessing some sort of natural phenomenon that has yet to be fully documented. The man relating the story above thought it at first was "ignis fatuus" or "foolish fire". The definition of this rare phenomenon is well-summed up by *Wikipedia*;

> "A will-o'-the-wisp, will-o'-wisp, or ignis fatuus; Medieval Latin for "foolish fire" is an atmospheric ghost light seen by travelers at night, especially over bogs, swamps or marshes. It resembles a flickering lamp and is said to recede if approached, drawing travelers from the safe paths. The phenomenon is known by a variety of names, including jack-o'-lantern, friar's lantern, hinkypunk (sic), and hobby lantern in English folk belief, well attested in English folklore and in much of European folklore."

The Mojave orbs or ghost lights seem to appear in the open desert as well as deep in mine shafts and rocky clefts, so we don't know if it's the same thing, but it sure sounds like what many people are reporting. Now this next article combines the paradoxical elements of a scientific explanation that might work for the desert (uranium deposits) but again with a decidedly paranormal twist (ghosts of dead miners). It's also from almost a hundred years later so people were still experiencing the "hoodoo" out in the Mojave just as old Buck said. It too comes from *The Desert Sun*, August 4th, 1955:

CHEAPER TO USE "GHOST LIGHT" TO

FIND URANIUM NOT GIEGER
COUNTER ADVISES OLIVER

San Bernardino Sun-Telegram. Those Geiger counter salesmen are going to be real mad about it but none other than the desert sage, Harry Oliver, says radioactive ore deposits can be seen better than they can be detected by electronic devices and a whole lot cheaper too."

Oliver, who is reputedly on friendly terms with the ghosts of countless desert prospectors, claims to have interviewed said ghosts and divulges their advice in the Summer "hot weather" number of his Desert Rat Scrap Book. Harry has even labeled the issue his "Ghost Town Packet" but spurns writing about any ghost towns that have failed to produce a fair quota of spirits. Back to the interviews, the ghosts at Ft. Oliver do the work for Harry. They call up shades of the great prospectors, and, presto, Harry has enough copy for his Ghost Town number. That is how he learned about the easier, cheaper and surer way to find uranium. It was told him by Shady Myrick's ghost at Randsburg and seconded by Jack Nosser's shade, the latter being a bit miffed at not getting the first interview. It seems that some 50 years back when the standard dictionaries were saying that uranium was relatively scarce but worthless metal, that the Mojave prospectors used to entertain themselves with the stuff around campfires. The only known use for radioactive substances was radium at that time and like "white spar" of the same period none knew or cared about such a thing as tungsten. Radioactive deposits were known by these old timers at several spots in the desert, chiefly in areas of volcanic activity.

In hot weather, and on nights when it was clear out without moonlight, came the phenomenon of "ghost light." Ghost light was known to all the old-timers. They loved to spin campfire yarns about it, particularly for the edification of tenderfeet. It took a fair-sized radioactive deposit to give off enough of the eerie ghostly light to be seen any considerable distance but there were spots around Randsburg, Granite Wells, Lavie, Cima and Kingston where such a show could be counted on most any summer night when it wasn't too dark. Oliver, who asserts he is being truthful, for the moment, thinks a convenient hill and a pair of binoculars will beat any scintilator (sic) in locating titanium. "Those ghost lights just don't show from low grade deposits," he says. The Thousand Palms publisher who combines his editing with the presidency of the Desert Rat Liars Club, advises "just ask an old timer where he has seen 'ghost light' and you are dead sure to locate uranium. Of course, the old timer may get there first if he suspects what you are after."

GHOSTS DISTURBED

Genuine Desert Ghost Town ghosts resent intrusion of jeeps and Geiger counters, so says Harry Oliver of Thousand Palms. Oliver is up with the old timer's method of finding radioactive ore and recalls how 'ghost light' can be seen on the desert at night. It is caused by uranium deposits Oliver asserts.

I'm not sure about the veracity of an article that contains reference to the "Desert Rat Liars Club", but some research on Harry Oliver, the source of the story turns up the fact he was a noted Hollywood set designer who loved the desert and edited the quarterly *Desert Rat Scrapbook*. He was known to love colorful stories which he combined with factual accounts, so take it for what it's worth.

But what about accounts of "orbs" or balls of light having a sense of intelligence or interaction with people? As this volume of my series only deals with the Mojave in California, I have but one story that claims that type of perceived behavior. It comes from a couple that were camping down near Joshua Tree National Park that claimed a "star-like" light kept appearing over their tent one night in the summer of 1997. Finding they could see some sort of bright purple light shining down on them through the thin fabric of their nylon tent, they stepped out to see what it was. Above them hung a brilliant ball or sphere of self-generating light, as stated purple in color, that was hanging there motionless about forty feet up. It was about "the size of an orange" and seemed to slowly pulsate in intensity. The husband stated that when they moved toward it to get a better view, it rose in the air as though conscious of their desire to get closer. For some reason the wife tried talking to it in a soothing tone that seemed to draw the light closer but when they yelled at it (apparently in frustration at it not coming close enough to examine) the ball of light would zoom far away and hang on the horizon. The whole thing sounds a bit crazy to be honest and the account ended with the couple deciding that the light must have been some sort of "UFO" because eventually it (or *they*) decided to end the encounter by flying away into the night sky and vanishing. Orb or spaceship? I put that one away in the "high strangeness" file but I offer it for consideration of the phenomenon.

Moving on from ghosts and orbs, we now come to another of the Mojave's mysteries that always generate a raised eyebrow or two – giants. And not the hairy giants of the Yucca Man or Cement Monster lore, but true giant humans of biblical proportions and abilities. It seems the desert has a long folklore of giant beings, going back to the legends and narratives of the early Native Americans, as evidenced by their beautiful and mysterious (to our modern eyes at least) rock art and carvings. Called geoglyphs or intaglios, and created by scraping away surface soil to show the darker rock or gravel beneath, they show large animals or humanoid figures marked out on the ground and often only completely visible from the air. In fact, many of the best-known ones were discovered by some of the first pilots flying over the desert way back in the 1930's. Anthropologists maintain these are connected to early creation myths and ceremony, but their true meaning has been unfortunately lost to the mists of time. At least to modern minds, as many of the remaining tribes still maintain some of their observances and rituals associated with their ancient beliefs but choose to keep and celebrate them in private. Which one has to admit is completely understandable considering how they have been treated over the centuries.

But with the coming of the white man, there also began a lore of actual giants, and though not too plentiful or well-documented, are among the accounts that interest me the most as they contain some of the most colorful and frankly, *bizarre* details imaginable. To get the ball rolling I have an article published on August 5th, 1947 in the *Madera Tribune:*

AGE OF GIANTS EVIDENCE FOUND

LOS ANGELES, Aug. 5. A band of amateur archeologists announced today that they have discovered a lost civilization of men nine feet tall in California caverns. Howard E. Hill, spokesman for the expedition, said the civilization may be "the fabled lost continent of Atlantis." The caves contain mummies of men and animals and implements of a culture 80,000 years old but "in some respects more advanced than ours," Hill said. He said the 32 caves covered a 180-square-mile area in California's Death Valley and southern Nevada. Professional archaeologists were skeptical of Hill's story. Los Angeles county museum scientists pointed out that dinosaurs and tigers, which Hill said lay side by side in the caves, appeared on earth 10,000,000 to 15,000,000 years apart.

There was also another article detailing more of this "most-amazing" find carried in *The San Diego Union:*

LOS ANGELES, Aug., 4 (AP)- A retired Ohio doctor has discovered relics of an ancient civilization, whose men were 8 or 9 feet tall, in the Colorado desert near the Arizona-Nevada-California line, an associate said today. Howard E. Hill, of Los Angeles, speaking before the Transportation Club, disclosed that several well-preserved mummies were taken yesterday from caverns in an area roughly 180 miles (sic) square, extending through much of southern Nevada from Death Valley, Calif., across the Colorado River into Arizona. Hill said the discoverer is Dr. F. Bruce Russell, retired Cincinnati physician, who stumbled on the first of several tunnels in 1931, soon after coming West and deciding to try mining for his health.

MUMMIES FOUND

Not until this year, however, did Dr. Russell go into the situation thoroughly, Hill told the luncheon. With Dr. Daniel S. Bovee, of Los Angeles - who with his father helped open up New Mexico's cliff dwellings - Dr. Russell has found mummified remains, together with implements of the civilization, which Dr. Bovee had tentatively placed at about 80,000 years old.

"These giants are clothed in garments consisting of a medium length jacket and trouser extending slightly below the knees," Hill said. "The texture of the material is said to resemble gray dyed sheepskin, but obviously, it was taken from an animal unknown today."

MARKINGS DISCOVERED

Hill said that in another cavern was found the ritual hall of the ancient people, together with devices and markings similar to those now used by the Masonic order. In a long tunnel were well preserved remains of animals, including elephants and tigers. So far, Hill added, no women have been found. He said the explorers believe that what they found was the burial place of the tribe's hierarchy. Hieroglyphics, he added, bear a resemblance to what is known of those from the lost continent of Atlantis. They are chiseled, he added, on carefully polished granite. He said Dr. Viloa V. Pettit, of London, who made excavations around Petra, on the Arabian desert, soon will begin an inspection of the remains.

Wow. There in these two articles we have not only giant humans, but mummies, dinosaurs, underground cities and the lost continent of Atlantis (which supposedly sank beneath the waves in the Aegean but in this account somehow ended up *under* Death Valley!). Now if you Google the term "Death Valley Giants" or "Death Valley Underground Cities" you will get a plethora of articles purporting to expand on the theme but most of them seem to be extensions or embroideries of these articles. I won't regurgitate them all here as they veer off into copious "theories" that include all manner of alien, illuminati and conspiracy folklore and I could not possibly do it justice in a single chapter in one book. Suffice it to say it all gets more fabulous and extreme in the retelling. If you really want to get a sampling of the original stories, you should try to find an old book titled *Death Valley Men* (MacMillan Company, N.Y. 1932), which was published in the 1930's and details the author's encounters with several prospectors and eccentrics who claimed to have discovered more lost tunnels and fabulous treasures connected with mysterious civilizations. Of course, no concrete proof is ever offered and all the informants seem to go missing or meet violent ends as is typical of these types of tales, but I guess that goes with the territory.

Now I do have a personal story to tell that includes all of these elements, which shows the ideas put forth in the old articles and books are still current in modern times. I was once hiking with a friend out in the Old Woman Mountains, a range near the lower end of the Mojave in California.

We had stopped for a water break while following an old mining road when we saw a real character coming along the trail toward us. He was dressed in rags, a headscarf covering most his features and using a long walking stick that had numerous religious symbols and ornaments dangling from it (crosses, half-moons, stars, etc.). Coming up to us we found this seemingly hoary old prophet was not an elderly Gandalf out on a fabulous mission, but actually a rather young man in his late twenties. He was friendly enough and after a bit of small talk about the heat, rattlesnakes and the like, he looked around (like anyone was going to overhear us out there) and in a low conspiratorial tone imparted his real purpose in being in such a remote spot.

His biblical "research" had led him to discover that the true Mount Zion and Mount Sinai were actually located in the Mojave Desert and that the whole "happened in the Middle East thing" was a mistranslation perpetrated by the Dark One's minions to mislead everyone. Although I badly wanted to point out the total absurdity of his geography at the very least, I just nodded attentively and listened. He went on to tell us that the last battle was going to be fought "real soon" out there because the giants who had formerly lived on the Earth, *the Nephilim*, had tired of living underground for the past few eons and had decided to come to the surface and wage war on man. When I asked what they had been living on or doing under the ground, he assured me that they had thousands of miles of tunnels connecting farms and living quarters that supplied their needs and wants deep in the earth, unknown to anyone except a select few. Then he added a last tidbit before moving along on his way – there were "bad people who worshiped the Devil" and had a compound deep within the mountains we were hiking and to be very careful if we kept going. Now if you've read the other chapters in this book, you know there really *are* more than a few nuts and "bad people" out in the Mojave into that sort of thing, so we did wonder if he might have seen something. But as to the other part of his wonderful "research" all we could do as he very nicely wished us well and ambled off was look at each other and go "Yep, there's *another* one." The desert is full of characters like this, and trust me, if you explore out there long enough you'll run into more than a few. It's part of my love and fascination with the place. But giants and underground cities? At least not on *that* trip.

Oh, and we didn't run into any Devil worshippers either.

That the desert's beauty and mysterious appeal often lies in the fact it can be so truly prehistoric and primitive looking is no surprise, so it should also come as no shock that some people have claimed it still holds relict populations of ancient flora and fauna.

But dinosaurs?

Of course, most of these accounts come from early explorers, from before a time when camera and satellite have opened up and exposed most unknown regions, but none the less are still quite fascinating. The late 1800's was a time when the science of paleontology was just maturing and the interest in the giant lizards of the past was becoming the subject of many popular books and newspaper articles. Take this early and quite fantastic one, from the August 5th edition of *The Sonoma Democrat*, 1876:

A DRAGON IN THE DESERT. THE STRANGE STORY OF A TRAVELER IN THE GREAT AMERICAS DESERT.

A correspondent of the Denver Paper says: I was traveling horseback along a stretch of country which, for a long distance, merits the appellation of the Great American Desert. As far as the eye could reach not a living thing or object created by the hand of man could be seen. On every side the horizon only bounded the view, and not even where the sky kissed the plain did aught but the scanty prairie grass, already burned to brown under the rays of the last Summering sun, lift itself, dotted here and there by innumerable cacti, from mother earth. Save the quickly recovering thud of my horse's hoofs as he loped over the prairie, not a sound was to be heard, and the stillness was profound. But the silence and the solitude were not for long. As I was about to seek a place to build a fire and bivouac for the night, suddenly a long trailing form started from the earth, and a queer rumbling cry was borne to my ears upon the Western wind. Hardly had the sound died upon the air when an intense trembling seized my horse, and, with distended nostrils and dilated eyes, he begun looking on all sides as if to find a way of escape.

And now the same strange cry was repeated, and my terrified sight perceived an enormous reptile, half serpent, half quadruped, that was now running, now creeping along the earth, with incredible rapidity. Although my limbs almost refused to perform their office for terror, I had turned mechanically to leap on my horse, notwithstanding that I knew that the pace at which the monster was coming was far faster than that of a horse at full gallop, but the beast had broken away from where I had tied him, and was quickly devouring the earth with rapid feet. Not, however, away from the coming danger. Although destruction stared me in the face, I almost lost consciousness of my peril in viewing the strange scene that followed.

As soon as the terrible thing perceived that the horse was able to run at a rate that compelled an inconvenient degree of speed to catch up with him, he suddenly stopped in his career, and for a moment remained silent and motionless, and the only sound to be heard was that made by the retreating horse, which was growing fainter and fainter. Immediately, ere it had become quite lost to the ear, the cause of the brute's flight begun to utter a sonorous roaring that one moment sounded like some brutish mother calling her young, and another a weird imitation of a cooing dove. Hardly had the sound been uttered, when the horse, which was now almost lost to sight in the rapidly growing darkness, stopped. Presently he turned around and begun with hastening steps to return. The noise still continued, and even to my human hearing seemed to have a pleading, inviting note in it.

The Brobdingnagian beast, too, had assumed the shape at once of a cat ready to play with her kittens, and of a serpent when trying to charm its prey into its folds. And now let me describe the monster. Like other saurians, it had the body of a lizard, uplifted on, as near as I could judge, eight feet, but its propelling power, as already noted, seemed to exist chiefly in its tail, which streamed behind the body at least a hundred feet. The trunk of the monster must have been thirty feet long by about half that figure in width, and at least from eight to ten feet through. The feet seemed little more than paddles with which to push this huge body along, and apparently had little supporting power, the creature's belly touching the ground except when its rapid motion forced it forward in the air. The head was flattened at the top, and towered high up over the body on a neck greater in diameter than a barrel, and fully ten feet in length. The eyes, as large as saucers, were about a yard and a half apart, and gleamed like lanterns on either side of a carriage. Thus far, the mouth was only partly open, to emit the sound above noted, so that in the comparative darkness I could not see it distinctly. The color was a dark purple, such as is sometimes used in churches at Lenten time, mottled with black.

By this time the horse had come within the embrace of the seducer, and the charming all at once ceased. Another movement, and the terrible mouth, which I could now see was as large as a barn door, opened, and a forked tongue darted out and pulled the poor beast within. Then came the sound of the teeth crunching and the breaking of bones, mingled with the stifled death cry of as faithful a brute as ever man bestrode. Then all was still, and the frightful creature lay motionless, as if digesting its meal. Presently it stirred, and, giving myself up for lost, I made up my mind to be its next victim, when, turning, it rapidly rolled away in the direction from which it came, without as much as looking at me. More dead than alive with terror, I made the best of my way to this place.

Okay, I think it's safe to say that account might have

been more the result of a bottle of the good stuff, than a real event, but the idea that giant lizards living out in the remote areas of the Mojave Desert might still survive had its constant expression in later, more nuanced articles as well. Here we have a fairly sober account from *The Los Angeles Herald* of May 19th, 1892:

WEIRD DESERT MONSTER

Prospectors in Search of a Gigantic Reptile Which Wears a Head Like a Cracker Box. It Is Over Thirty Feet Long - Makes a Track in the Sand Eighteen Inches Across - Its Trail About Newbery and Hazlett.

George Nay, the well-known mining man, for fifteen years a resident of the Needles, on the Colorado river, is at the Grand hotel, San Francisco, and tells a remarkable story of the discovery of a strange monster in the vicinity of Daggett.

Mr. Nay stopped at Daggett twenty-four hours on his way up. A party of prospectors headed by E. W. Spear had just arrived. Spear reported the finding of a curious trail eighteen inches wide in the sand of the desert, twenty miles toward Death Valley from Daggett. He followed the strange trail for some distance, when suddenly turning almost at right angles around a sand dune he beheld a monstrous reptile, or animal, at least thirty feet long, with a head, so he expressed it, "larger than a candle box" and "eyes as big as teacups" and luminous in their brightness. Spear was alone, and being scared ran for camp as fast as his legs could take him. When he had told his story, he was greeted with loud laughter, for nobody believed it. Next day, however, Henry Brown, who was coming across the desert in the lead of another party, saw it. Both reported it at Daggett. The Daggett people had taken no stock in Spear's story, although he was always known as a truthful man. They thought, however, he was trying to play a practical joke on them. He stoutly persisted, however, that he had really seen the strange monster. When Brown arrived the next day, and corroborated it in every detail and added particulars as to how it appeared, they remembered having seen curious trails in the sand over the Atlantic and Pacific track thereabout for two years past. Also that these trails were particularly numerous between Newbery and Haslett, nearby stations on the Atlantic and Pacific. The greatest interest prevailed, and at once a party was organized to go and search for the monster, be it snake or some surviving specimen of a supposed long-extinct desert animal resembling one, and only found now in the large museums. Horses and pack animals were at once secured. Two cowboys were among the party, and they took out with them a number of riatas, intending to ride close enough, if safe to do so, to lariat the monster and take him alive. It was the intention to exhibit him at the world's fair. Mr. Nay says the people of Daggett are fully convinced that there is some monster of the kind set forth loose on the Mojave Desert, and they fully expect that the party they have outfitted will secure it.

Its trail looks almost exactly as if a sack of grain or ore had been dragged through the sand. What the unique denizen of the desert lives on is not known."

A little bit more believable in both the monster's size and scope, I have a string of articles that seem to follow the same case. Witness the follow-up in *The Herald* just five days later:

A LIVING LOST LINK

A Supposed Iguanodon Benrissantensis. A Prehistoric Monster in Death Valley Desert. The Horrible Creature Recently Seen by a Scientist - Its Description of an Animal Belonging; to Past Ages.

That marvelous monster which was seen in the Death Valley desert, about twenty miles from Daggett, recently by Mr. E. W. Speer and Mr. Henry Brown of Daggett, at separate times, while out on prospecting parties, has occasioned a wonderful interest in scientific circles, especially those who have made paleontological research. Yesterday Mr. Oscar W. Clark, who has been spending some time in

Daggett and who has been making geological researches along the coast in the interest of the Royal Academy of Sciences, was on his way to Coronado to take a rest. Mr. Clark has made a number of journeys into Death Valley desert, and was one of the parties who saw this gigantic monster. He has sent the result of his experiences to the Smithsonian Institute, with a view to having a party sent out here to endeavor to capture the monster.

"The announcement of the experiences of Messrs. Spear and Brown rather anticipated me," said Mr. Clark yesterday. "I had a fine opportunity of seeing this strange denizen of that mysterious land known as Death Valley desert, and I desire to say that this animal is the most wonderful living proof of the exact authenticity of the researches made by savants into the field of paleontological study. This animal is really the only living link between prehistoric times and the present. It is virtually a marvel of the ages, an eighth wonder of the world. A marvelous illustration of the profound economy of nature.

It was six weeks ago that I had the pleasure of seeing this remarkable animal. I was some thirty miles distant from Daggett, and stopped at 6 o'clock in the evening to rest, having made some valuable additions to my collection of fossil remains. Happening to glance to the southwest through the haze heat peculiar to the desert I saw a strange body moving along about one mile away. I went toward it and was soon both elated and horrified by seeing an animal fully thirty feet long that differed from any of the known forms of the present epoch. It was an immense monster, walking part of the time on its hind feet and at times dragging itself through the sand, and leaving tracks of a three-toed foot and a peculiar scratchy configuration in the sand whenever it changed its form of locomotion and dragged itself. The forelimbs of the animal were extremely short, and it occasionally grasped the desert scrub and devoured it. The thumb of the three-pronged forefoot was evidently a strong conical spine that would be a dangerous weapon to attack. Whenever the animal stood upright it was fully fourteen feet high. The head was as large as a good-sized cask, and was shaped somewhat like a horse, while the body was as large as that of an elephant, with a long tail extending from the hindquarters much like that of an alligator.

When I saw it, the strange animal was on the edge of a great sinkhole of alkaline water —a sink-hole, by the way, that my guides told me was a bottomless pit, and evidently a remnant of the days when Death Valley was an inland sea. I approached within 300 yards of the monster, crawling cautiously over the sand and watched it for fully half an hour. Suddenly the beast began to bellow, and the sound was of a most terrifying and blood-curdling character. Its. immense eyes, fully as large as saucers, projected from the head, and gleamed with a wild and furious fire, while from the enormous mouth of the monster streams of steam-like vapor were exhaled, and as they drifted toward one the effluvia was (sic) something awful. The animal was liver color, with bronze-like spots.

The monster dragged itself to the edge of the sink hole and lashed its tail, and finally fell off into a quiescent condition. I left the scene and attempted to secure the assistance of my guides in an effort to capture the monster, but they were absolutely terrified and refused to do anything. From what I saw of the animal I am perfectly satisfied that it is one of the species of the Iguanodon Bennissantenis, of the European Jurassic, an animal presenting many points of structure in common with the iguana of today. In fact, that is the report that I have sent in, and knowing fully well the geologic environments of the Pacific slope and the very remarkable and peculiar conditions regarding the Death Valley section, I am satisfied that my deductions are correct, and that there is today living and existing in the desert of Death Valley one of the most remarkable animals now existing on the face of the globe, none other than one of the monsters of the pre-historic epoch—a wonder of the centuries."

Now here we have a "famous scientist" claiming that he too saw the animal and was close enough to note that the "effluvia was something awful". In other words, it had horrible breath! And while efforts were supposed to have been put into effect to capture this magnificent beast, somehow it never was brought to heel. The last traces I find of "Iguanodon Bennissantenis" in Death Valley comes from *The Coronado Mercury* of June 4th, 1892 and is but a brief re-cap:

> A scientist who has been in Death Valley says he has seen the desert monster and believes it to be one of the species of the Iguanodon Bennissantensis, of the Jurassic age, the only living specimen of the animal life of the prehistoric epoch. It is thirty feet long, fourteen feet high, and a combination of horse and alligator in appearance.

But is there a giant species of lizard still living in Death Valley or the surrounding Mojave that has yet to be discovered? I doubt it as the largest current inhabitant, the Chuckwalla or Sauromalus ater as he's known to science grows to only about eighteen inches long at most. They can become quite fat and round, but as they eat mostly plants and wildflowers I can hardly see one dining on horse flesh or lone prospectors. I often see one sunning itself on a rock or outcropping when traveling through the Mojave.

Moving on from living dinosaurs, we come to something that sends a chill down almost everyone's spine – huge spiders! I have several accounts in my files, both historic and modern concerning huge arachnids being encountered out in the Mojave, as well as a short personal one. I'll start with my own "encounter", but have to preface it with the disclaimer it was an ordinary tarantula, abet a very large one.

I was camping out one night in August, under a full moon and just when the tarantula mating season was getting started. For those who are not familiar with the habits of these huge spiders, suffice it to say that in the fall the males come out at night and go in search of receptive females to breed with, often wandering the whole night across the open desert floor. In some places, you might see a trail of them crossing a remote road or trail, looking like a procession of black hairy nightmares as they lumber along checking every nook and cranny for a mate.

So, as I lay there on my cot, enjoying the bluish light of the moon illuminating the desert around me, I was lost in thought when I happened to be looking at the ground before me where I had set my cooler down from the back of the jeep. Suddenly from behind the cooler came an absolutely huge tarantula ambling across the sand. I watched bemused as he came right over to the front leg of my cot, then proceeded to examine my flip-flops with his huge hairy forelegs, turning them about as he seemingly tried to make sense of what they were and could possibly be used for. After a few moments of inquiry, he then made his way over to the rock ring I had made to kindle a fire and cook over, probing each opening in the stones to see if a female of his species lurked within. I should point out this was also an excellent example of why you never leave your boots or shoes flat on the ground when you go to sleep out in the desert as you never know what will decide to come investigate or take shelter inside.

The big spider then proceeded to curl up by the warm rocks and lay still for a while, drawing his thick legs up until he resembled a large furry black tennis ball. Getting up and donning my flip-flops, I grabbed my phone and tried to get some video of the monster. Pulling out my flashlight, I lit him up and the minute the bright light hit him the big guy came to life and tried to escape back into the darkness. I stood still as he ran straight at the tips of my feet before making a right turn and heading back into the large jumble of boulders nearby, capturing it all on my phone. I'm going to upload it to my YouTube channel eventually so you can see how big the old boy actually was, probably the largest tarantula I've ever seen out in the wild.

And thankfully, completely harmless.

Now in days gone by, some claimed the large spiders would attack them without provocation, sometimes in mass and with deadly intent. I've got a great account in the files from *The Los Angeles Herald* of January 26th, 1908:

ABOUT TARANTULAS

The great spider called the "tarantula," whose entire surroundings are so full of interest, is justly an object of dread to man and beast. Latin names for the creature have been bountifully supplied, and it is somewhat difficult to decide which are most deserving. The title of "Mygale Hentzii" seems to fit the Arizona variety tolerably well.

The Mygale sometimes spreads over six-inches square, but more frequently four to five inches. A shaggy coat of hair covers the surface of the great spider. It is supplied with six strong, bony legs and two dangerous pedipapa or strikers, each armed with a sharp sting and poison sac. The strikers are frequently mistaken for two front legs, and from this arises the idea that the creature has stings on its feet.

Two powerful projections, resembling

jaws, protrude from the head. Under each of these is a curved poison fang, similar to a cat's claw, but longer (exactly like those of a rattlesnake), which may be lifted, extended and hooked into the victim. A person thus stung or bitten must cut the tarantula away at once for the spider does not seem willing to unhook its fangs.

There are two varieties. The large, black, so-called "Texas" tarantula, a fierce and quarrelsome species, and a somewhat smaller kind, brown, heavier built and less aggressive.

The hair surrounding the mouth of the tarantula is of crimson color. The creature must be turned on its back to see this.

The venomous tarantula, in spite of all discussions to the contrary, does build and live in the regular "Trap-door-spider" nest. There seems to be an idea that the trap-door spider is harmless, which is certainly erroneous. It uses no web net, easily capturing its prey by extraordinary springs.

Those who have seen this arachnidan by daylight can have little idea of its power and fleetness. During the day it moves slowly and clumsily in the dazzling light, but when darkness comes it can move with ease and certainty.

Credible accounts have appeared stating that the tarantula can leap sixteen feet. Repeated statements have credited it with leaps of three feet or more. In the year 1870, or near that date, three men disturbed several tarantula nests in San Diego. They were immediately attacked by the huge spiders, and had to run for their lives, taking refuge in the waters of the bay.

It is almost impossible for one who isn't well-informed to locate the tarantula's eyes. But it has eyes—six almost invisible specks no larger than the point of a pin, mounted on a tiny setting that glows out of the back. Two peer forward, two sideways and two behind. The head and trunk, by the way, are all one piece.

Tarantulas are considered deadly foes to each other, and are seldom found in company. When imprisoned together there is a fight; one succumbs and is eaten by the victor.

Nature has done a service in making the tarantula so hideous and formidable a looking object. Indeed, it is owing to this repulsiveness that no greater number of persons are stung. The sight of the great, hairy spider crawling nearby will cause a cold, creeping sensation down the back of almost any one.

The Mygale poison is of a fearful nature, more dreaded than that of a rattlesnake, and unless very slightly scratched, and heroic measures used, the result is fatal. Many deaths are recorded, caused by these spiders.

The Mexicans claim that in Mexico an extract is made from the tarantula and taken internally as medicine. This may be so. Many blood poisons may be taken into the stomach in small doses with very little ill effect. The bee sting, for instance, is painful; but the same poison gives honey its agreeable flavor.

The spider itself, when stung by another immediately dies, and it may be easily killed by administrations of poison internally, such as cyanide; even gelsemium (sic) and other fluid extracts are effective.

The deadly foe of the tarantula is the "tarantula hawk." It is a giant blue wasp, with fiery wings, and they seem never to be at rest. With tireless energy they fly and walk rapidly along the ground, running into every crevice and hole, and examining every suspicious object—after the dreaded tarantula.

The fate of the giant spider once discovered by the hawk is both certain and attended with fascinating horror.

The winged insect hovers over the victim until it finds a good opportunity to sting. The poison acts in a peculiar manner, the tarantula becoming paralyzed. In this state the eggs of the hawk are laid in the helpless spider, who remains alive to be slowly devoured by the hungry larvae.

I love the fact that "credible accounts have appeared stating that the tarantula can leap sixteen feet," or that men were attacked by nests of the giant spiders and forced to flee for their lives in this colorful old article. The idea of the big spiders being vicious and out for human blood is one that has resulted in some pretty hilarious horror movies, usually with arachnids of fabulous size.

But what if there were/are giant spiders out there much bigger than we currently accept? I have an email from a woman who lives out in the Mojave near the town of

Baker, California who claims that one night while coming home from running some errands she witnessed something on a remote road that truly is the stuff of nightmares.

Kay R. is a mother of three and works as a rural mail carrier, so she's familiar with most of the desert animals one might see along the roads at night.

"I was coming home from the store, going along Powerline toward my turnoff when I saw it. I was coming up to a small hill and slowed down because sometimes you meet quad riders coming the other way and the road turns pretty sharp there. It was maybe around 7:30 and it was just getting dark. So I as I came up to the top I saw what I thought was a dead rabbit or something on the side of the road with what I also first thought was a dog or coyote pulling at it. I could just see the top of the thing's body through the bits of grass.

But when I got closer I saw whatever it was back onto the road pulling the rabbit and immediately I went "oh, my God, it's a spider!" I mean it's butt was the size of a football! Just huge. All black and hairy. Couldn't believe it. I stopped dead and watched it try to pull this dead rabbit onto the road out of the grass. I was in my truck so I thought maybe I'd zoom forward and squish it good but before I could put my foot on the gas the thing jumped forward and scuttled into the grass again. I pulled up and leaned over in my seat to look out the passenger side to see if I could see it on the grass but couldn't. Even took my flashlight out and shined it all over the side of the road but nothing. After a few minutes, I drove away. No way I was going to get out and look. But I saw it. My sister says my eyes were probably tired and I saw a fox or something, but I know. I saw it!

Oh, and the next day when I came back the rabbit was gone so whether it came back and got it, I don't know."

Kay writes that she still passes that spot almost every day when making her mail rounds but has yet to see the monster again. I'm not sure what to think as I too have been tired driving along and thought I've seen something only to have it be revealed as a fence post or some other piece of debris by the road. I think we all have. But she was adamant that she clearly saw the rear end and hairy legs of a huge black spider. Now something with the "butt the size of a football" would have to be at least three feet across and that would certainly qualify as a genuine monster in anyone's book. And if that beastie is out there, I can only hope he never comes crawling about my camp at night!

The other oft-repeated story of giant spiders in the Mojave concerns what is termed "the camel spider". A large member of the Solifugae family, it is also called "the sun spider" or "wind scorpion" and is the subject of many desert horror stories. If you Google "camel spider" you will undoubtedly see pictures of them alongside our soldiers in Iraq and other parts of the mid-east, and often credited with being of tremendous size and ferocity. Most are Photoshop hoaxes, but the creatures are real enough and native to the Mojave Desert as well. In fact, anyone who lives here will tell you they find them in the house and surrounding yards all the time. They look absolutely fierce and scary with their massive front jaws and fangs, but in truth they are quite harmless unless you seriously mess with one. I've had them run up my leg when out camping (they're really fast) and even found one in the house that I saw clamber out of one of the pockets on my backpack after returning from a desert trip, but have never been bitten. During the summer months, I often like to sit out back on my porch and watch them chase after beetles and other insects drawn by the yard lights as they sweep them up in their long front legs and zoom off to enjoy their struggling meal somewhere in the darkness. But I certainly would not want to be bit by one, as those massive jaws look painful.

But yet I've heard the stories of how soldiers in the Middle East would see huge ones that got their name "camel spider" from the "fact" they were seen jumping up and ripping at the exposed bellies of camels and bringing them down by disemboweling the poor animal. Or that they would be found, a foot or more in length, nestled down in some unlucky serviceman or woman's sleeping bag, waiting in the folds to deliver a painful bite. And now of course, they have been imported into the Mojave by hiding in the shipping containers being returned to the Marine bases from overseas deployments. Scary and somewhat plausible except for the fact the harmless and certainly beneficial insects (they love to eat cockroaches) have always been native to the Mojave Desert.

And while they can grow to be five inches in length, no one has ever captured or photographed any of the foot-long or more monsters rumored to have been unwittingly imported by the Marines.

At least not yet.

So, let's move from the sun spider to one that I'd never heard of until I came across this old article from *The Los Angeles Herald* of April 17th, 1911; the dreaded Whiskey Spider!

HELP! MAN WAS NOT DRUNK; 'WHISKY SPIDER' BIT HIM

Desert Insect Said to Cause Delirium Tremens Symptoms

SAN BERNARDINO, April 16 - Sentenced to the county jail for intoxication Louis Hansen, a miner, is now believed to have been bitten by a "whisky spider," a rare pest that makes its home in the water holes of the desert.

The bite of the insect produces the same effects as accompany delirium tremens. It is said. Hansen was found on the desert on the outskirts of Ludlow, digging in the sand. He had every appearance of being in the last stages of a protracted spree. The justice of the peace gave him a ten-day sentence to sober him up, and he was brought to the county jail here yesterday by Constable Button.

Today he recovered his senses for the first time in a week. Louis says that he was working in the Cucamonga hills, sinking a drift, and a week ago he went to the spring and stooped down to take a drink of water. That is the last he remembers, he says. In a week's time he crossed the mountains and made his way to Ludlow, but how he did so he does not know. He claims that he has not touched liquor for months. He says he is positive that he was bitten by the whisky spider.

I would venture to say that the "whiskey spider", if it ever existed, was more likely a Black Widow, and the serious complications the old miner was experiencing came from the effects of its toxic but not often fatal bite.

But you have to admit it is one of more inventive excuses I've ever heard offered to the court to excuse one's drunkenness. Might have to remember that one next time I decide to go on a "protracted spree".

The last mystery I'm going to deal with in this chapter concerns a caveman. A real caveman. But not a prehistoric one. His name was Frank Kritzer, or Critzer, and he actually lived in a cave hollowed out under a very famous Mojave paranormal location – Giant Rock. As I've covered in other chapters of this book, Giant Rock down near Landers, California was once a Native American ceremonial site, a beacon to early desert settlers and the official landing and gathering spot for UFO enthusiasts during the late 1940's and early 1950's. It got its alien connection when former Hughes Aircraft test-pilot George Van Tassel claimed that one night as he slept at the base of the nearly seven-story boulder, a flying saucer came down and beamed the blueprints for the "Integraton" (also detailed in this book) into his head.

But all that that was after Frank Kritzer was already dead, the victim of a mysterious suicide and murder attempt that still baffles people to this day. You see, for a few years prior to the start of World War Two, the strange man had been living under the giant boulder in a three-room cave "house" he had fashioned for himself. At the time the flat area surrounding Giant Rock was frequently used by desert pilots as a stopover or by Army pilots as an emergency landing strip in the high desert. Mr. Kritzer would often supply gasoline and various sundries to the visiting fliers for a price. But prior to 1941, the local authorities had also begun to suspect that the strange man was responsible for a series of thefts involving dynamite and other material from various remote mining locations in the area. Reports also came in of "strange lights or flares" being seen over Giant Rock, some as far away as the Army glider school over in Twentynine Palms, a distance of about twenty miles.

What could have this guy been up to?

Well, with the outbreak of hostilities in Europe, and Kritzer's obvious Germanic name, rumors started to fly. Was he a spy? A saboteur? Or "merely" a thief who was stealing dynamite and explosives from miners? And what could he be doing with all those explosives if not planning something nefarious?

The FBI got involved. The mysterious caveman was put under surveillance and his rock hollow home even searched but nothing was turned up. But then another huge cache of dynamite and gasoline was looted from a nearby mining operation as well as a local train depot and again suspicion fell upon the strange desert hermit. It was decided that three local officers from the Sheriff's department would make a call upon Kritzer on behalf of the FBI and see if they could find evidence of his crimes. So in July of 1942, the three officers drove out to Giant Rock to interview the caveman. Arriving at the door of his underground home, they identified themselves as officers of the law - and then without warning or reason Kritzer decided to bring down the curtain on the whole strange story.

He touched off a massive blast of dynamite that blew himself and most of his rocky home to bits, but miraculously didn't kill the three officers. Severely injured, but alive, the three managed to summon help and were rescued, but the caveman was no more. He had been pretty much vaporized by the explosion he had set off. A further search of the ruins turned up an additional 170 pounds of explosives, all stolen, that had been also wired to blow but thankfully hadn't detonated or it would have certainly killed the three policemen and more than likely destroyed Giant Rock.

People still don't know why he did it, or what the mysterious hermit was really up to, but all manners of extravagant theories have been advanced:

He was a Nazi sympathizer.

He was building a UFO base.

He planned on blowing Giant Rock to atoms because it was a portal or vortex for powers unknown.

Or just maybe, as some have suggested, he like many a strange desert hermit or character was suffering from what this old article appearing in *The Sacramento Union* of March 2nd, 1913 calls "desert madness":

SLAYER, 75, FREED ON PLEA OF "DESERT MADNESS"

SAN BERNARDINO, March I.—Jailed twice for the murder of J. C. Steiner, an "innocent bystander," killed in a revolver fight at Kramer in the desert a year ago. John Blake, aged 75 years, a veteran of the Sepoy revolt in India in 1858, was freed today, after the jury had disagreed. Judge Oster of the superior court discharged the aged man, expressing the belief that he was a victim of "desert madness." Steiner was killed by a shot which Blake had fired at W. J. Young, who was contesting a mining claim against Steiner.

Who knows?

In the end, I think he was just another one of those eccentric characters anyone who explores the great Mojave Desert encounters from time to time. An individual who decides to break contact with the ordinary world and pursue an existence in accordance to beliefs only they can comprehend or understand. I know I have run into them often enough, some harmless, others armed and decidedly dangerous.

And I'm more than sure there are many such eccentrics out there yet to be discovered. It's what gives exploring in the Mojave it's spice. You just never know *what* you're going to encounter!

Some Final Interesting Mojave Desert Oddities

In this chapter I have collected together a nice cross section of some interesting and perplexing topics I lump together under what I like to call "desert oddities", something that just leaves you scratching your head. Some venture into the paranormal and supernatural range, while others have a more rational or conventional explanation, but are still rather bizarre and of course, always interesting.

The first one up concerns something that desert backpackers or hikers have encountered on rare occasions and I bet wondered with furrowed brow as to the real purpose. If you're in the deserts of the Southern US (and in some places across the great plains too) you might have come across a giant cement arrow on some mountain ridge or out in the middle of nowhere. Looking exactly like a huge signpost or parking arrow set into the ground, these strange yet entirely human constructions make no sense to one on foot, as you cannot even see them unless standing almost directly on it. But that's entirely the point to these markings, they're not supposed to be followed by someone on foot, they are for guiding people flying overhead. You see, in the 1920's and early 1930's, the state of cross-country air travel and mail delivery was in its infancy. Pilots didn't have the aid of radar or air control tracking stations to guide them as they flew along for long fatiguing hours on end. And being in rather primitive planes, they didn't fly at that high of an altitude as they tried to navigate their way along by using ground landmarks like rivers, roads and mountain ranges. It was hard and dangerous work, but these early pilots were a dedicated and hardy lot. So, some bright lad somewhere came up with the simple yet brilliant idea of marking the flight paths they were to follow by placing giant cement arrows on the ground. They are basically road maps for pilots to use who had to navigate their path visually as they soared along. Many can still be found. For a treat, here is something you can do next time you're online. Go to Google Maps and type in this coordinate (35 04 39.19664 -116 23 30.73359) then switch to "earth view" and zoom in all the way. What you'll see is one of these cement arrows at the top of a small mountain right alongside the I-15 running through the Mojave just past Barstow, California. At the time of their use the arrows also had a beacon light and in some cases a small radio transmitter, but after being decommissioned by government in the late 1930's most of the equipment was stripped away and the remaining cement arrow left to crumble back into the desert. But as most things take centuries to disintegrate in the desert, many can still be seen today. I wonder what people a few hundred years from now will make of them? I'm sure some pretty fantastic theories will be proffered, everything from buried treasure to secret locations as we humans love to attach the most fanciful attributes to some pretty mundane objects.

Our next oddity is just such an example – if the current explanation for it is true! Out in the Mojave, in the Crucero Hills (just at the western tip of the Mojave National Preserve) at the top of a high ridge you will find a well-fabricated but rusting iron tube or telescope shaped object carefully set into the top of the rocks. It is in an area that is quite remote and other than a few mining operations and an old railroad bed, seemingly in the middle of nowhere that would give any possible hint to its purpose. Resembling a jet or possible rocket engine, and set carefully on two supporting "springs" or legs, it sits rusting away in the searing hot sun. Since its discovery (or more accurately *re-discovery*) it has been christened with the nickname of either "The Mojave Megaphone" or "Mojave Telescope" it has fascinated the hardy desert adventurer for years. And all sorts of fabulous explanations have been proposed for it. Some say it's a sighting device to show the way to a fabulous lost mine or secret cache or treasure trove. Others have postulated that it is some device cunningly fashioned to focus the wind or natural energy at the spot to create a vortex or portal. And of course, it wouldn't be complete without an alien or UFO association although it's obviously been welded and bolted together by the hand of man.

So, what is it?

The most recent and logical explanation is the rather mundane and ordinary interpretation that it's the horn or bell for a now-missing siren of some sort. Probably used by a mining or railroad company to alert their workers to a shift change or blasting session. Another solution along the same lines is that it was a siren that the Army used while conducting desert drills, tests or exercises in the area. A good mystery dashed? Perhaps, but there is still the chance someone will come along in the future and reveal it to be something completely different from the what is now currently believed to be the true purpose of the mysterious device. I will include a coordinate that will get you close, but be aware you will not see anything on any online satellite map as it is only about six feet long. Much too small to see clearly. Here it is (35 0.389, -116 11.941).

And another thing, it is pretty rough country so don't go out there without being properly prepared and familiar with desert travel.

I like the next little bit of Mojave lore as it fits nicely with a favorite device of every western and fantasy writer – the hole or formation in a high peak that shows the spot where to find something spectacular when the sun (or moon) shows through at a certain time of the day or year. Author supreme Jules Verne used the idea in his classic *Journey to the Center of the Earth*, where the leader of the expedition,

Professor Lindenbrock, uses the pointer shadow of a high peak in an Icelandic volcanic crater to show his comrades the entrance to the tunnels that lead underground. And so, in the Mojave we have numerous stories of such "pointers" or "gunsights". One of my favorites has been dubbed the "Shaman's Eye in the Sky" and is located in the Mojave National Preserve at coordinates (35 22.351, -115 48.310).

Created by the eroding away of softer rock around the lava core of an old volcano, the Shaman's Eye makes a perfect open hole in a ridge at the very top of the peaked formation. Said to be an ancient Native American ceremonial site, it has a long and colorful history. I unfortunately do not have any verifiable Native American accounts, but I do have two interesting stories from visitors and as usual, they differ remarkably. The first, from an older gentleman I met down near the Kelso Depot in the Preserve, contains all the elements of your classic "lady in white" or "lady of the lake" type legend. His telling me of his experience had been prompted by observing me reading a map on the hood of my jeep in preparation for getting some footage of the eye.

He had been camping near there one summer back in the 1960's and didn't even know of the "eye" until late one day when he noticed the sun shining through the opening and casting an almost perfect circle on the ground near his vehicle. Seeing that there was a "beautiful star-like" appearance to the sunlight as it streamed through the rock orifice, he wanted to try and get a picture. Fumbling for his camera, he just had it in hand when he saw the sun moving in its arc through the sky was about to leave the eye and ruin the shot. He was just focusing his lens when he said he heard a strange whistling sound and when he turned around saw a very beautiful "Indian gal" dressed almost entirely in white doe skins walking toward him holding a white owl feather. The man said he suddenly felt "drunk or out of it" and almost in a dream-like state as the maiden began to speak to him in perfect English. She told him he was in a very holy area and that she was the "spirit of the place" and would grant him long life and happiness but only if he left without taking pictures and swore never to reveal its location. Then, like all spectral visitations or ghostly apparitions, she simply vanished before his eyes and he "woke up, still standing there with my camera in my hand." Deciding he was going to follow her advice, he left without a shot and never told anyone else about the occurrence until a few years later when he felt more at ease about it.

I asked him if the maiden's promise ever came true, but he just shrugged and said "... never made any real money, but I'm married to a good woman and got no complaints."

Before I could ask more his wife, the "good woman" yelled at him to get back in the car as they were leaving and to quit "yakking to strangers." He gave me a wink and departed. Was he pulling my chain? I don't know, but he seemed earnest enough, although there are some seriously problematic elements to his story. The biggest one is that the Native Americans in the Mojave didn't wear "doe skins" like he described, that's a more Plains and Eastern tribe thing. They dressed very sparsely and with the coming of trade with the Spanish and later whites, very quickly adopted cotton and woven fabrics with long sleeves and flowing dresses. And why would "she" care about him telling anyone in the twentieth century about the location of the formation when it had been known for over a hundred years and well documented? Maybe the old guy was just trying to spice up my coming visit? But I do know the idea of a spiritual "guardian or defender" of holy places is so common in every culture that I give you the story for the price I got it.

Now our next account of the spot is radically different

in both its tone and message. Ryan K. is a hunter and was after game in the Preserve (you can still hunt there in strict accordance with Fish and Game Department rules) when he found himself camped down near the Shaman's Eye. He knew of the lore of the site and being a rather hard-boiled and cynical character considered all the tales and stories he had heard about it to be "total bullsh-t."

Until one cold night in December.

"Yeah, I was sleeping in the back of my truck just off the road by the eye. Went to bed early and wrapped up in my bag because it was biting cold and the wind was picking up. I'd been asleep for maybe an hour or so when I woke up suddenly. It was like I heard something but couldn't hear it when I opened my eyes. I sat up to look around, didn't see anything, and was just about to lie back down when I thought I saw someone standing at the front of my truck. Like a black shadow or just the outline of someone. The moon wasn't out so it was pretty dark and I couldn't really be sure because when I looked closer I didn't see anyone. Nothing. I figured it was just a mistake. I laid back down and closed my eyes and was just about asleep, or half-asleep when it felt like something brushed the top of my head! I had the sleeping bag pulled up pretty tight with just the top of my head sticking out and it felt like a rag getting pulled over my head or like when you walk through a spider web, you know? Man, I instantly was awake and sitting up, looking around.

About thirty feet away, just to the left of me I saw what looked like a tall shape standing in the scrub. Just an outline, shadow, but definitely looked like something or someone standing there. I couldn't tell if they were facing me or looking away but it definitely felt like they were staring at me. I just got this prickly feeling all over, like something is wrong or dangerous. I sleep with a pistol by my head so you know I had it in my hand. I even said "I have a gun" out loud, but didn't see any reaction. I reached down and grabbed my flashlight while keeping my eyes on the shape and got ready to light them up. Now here's the first really weird thing – I flipped on the light and shined it on the "person" or whatever – there was nothing there! Nothing but brush and a few small bushes. I swept the light all over but couldn't see anything, or where someone might had dropped down to the ground and was hiding. Nothing. I wondered if I had just imagined the shape but I was sure I saw something. I turned off the light but now my night vision was totally screwed so for a few seconds I couldn't really see shit. Looking again, I couldn't see anything and I flicked the light on and off for several times trying to see if I could catch something moving out there but didn't see a thing. After about a half hour of this crap I decided to lay back down and go back to sleep because I was pretty sure I was just freaking myself out now and there was nothing really out there.

It was quiet too. And while lying there with my eyes closed I couldn't hear anything moving, so after a little bit, maybe twenty minutes I fell back asleep. Then I had the worst crazy nightmare. I can't remember much of it now but it was like when you were a little kid and would dream about a monster or something chasing you and you couldn't run fast enough, or you were cornered and couldn't wake up. Just went on and on. Scared the shit out of me and when I did finally wake up I even heard myself make a little groan or cry. It took me a second to remember where I was and relax. I decided to get up and take a piss and smoke a cigarette or two. Got out of the truck and yes, I had my gun with me while I took care of things. I smoked and sat on the tailgate for a little while, just listening to the wind and a few owls in the distance. Finally, I just crawled back into my bag and went back to sleep.

Now here's the really troubling part. When I got up in the morning, just as the sun was coming up, I unzipped and got out to go to the bathroom again. It was light enough to see all around and when I came back I walked up to the side door of my truck to get something to eat out of the cooler. I was looking at the ground too, just to see if there were any tracks or prints so I could reassure myself that I hadn't really seen anything standing there in the night. There was nothing so I thought "Yep, just as I thought" when I happened to look up at the hood and froze. Right in the middle of my hood was a fist-sized rock, just sitting there like someone had placed it. I mean they had to have because it wasn't there when I went to bed and I certainly didn't do it. I looked around to see if anyone was watching before I reached for it, but the sun was up now and I didn't see a thing for miles. The rock wasn't anything special, not a certain shape or anything, just a hunk of blackish lava from the base of the eye. But just big enough to let me know someone had been there while I slept. But no tracks? I know an owl didn't drop it and if someone had thrown it I would have heard it dent the hood or seen some scratches. I was like "okay, I'm out of here" and not in the mood to play games with whoever was out there. I say "who" and not "what" as I'm not big on ghosts and that shit, but it was definitely totally weird and I was lucky someone didn't slit my throat when I was sleeping if they were that light and stealthy on their feet.

And I did feel something touch my head when I was in my bag, so yeah, I packed up and got the fuck out of Dodge."

Is the Shaman's Eye haunted? Or is it as many claim the spot of a vortex or multi-dimensional portal that still exerts some sort of power over those who visit? As I stated above, it's a theme beloved to all fantasy authors and I have to admit to loving the idea it shows the way to something cool and mysterious. And the thought that it has stood there silently for hundreds of thousands of years casting its magical "eye of light" on the ground makes the lore around it all the more impressive. Surely the early tribes surrounding it must have felt its power and effect in their belief systems, it's such a natural symbol of wonder. I'd love to find out more about their early stories and will continue to see if I can find out any additional information. In the meantime, if you visit the eye do so with an open mind.

Our next bit of desert bizarro happens to be down in Joshua Tree National Park and is an old favorite of mine. It's called "The Iron Door Cave" and has been the subject of much speculation and sensationalism as to its true function and purpose. Located at coordinates (34 01.248, -116 09.911) just to the west and rear of the Hidden Valley Campground, the site consists of a huge boulder under which a room has been walled off and now shut by very heavy duty iron door. Near the personal property of one of the park's most famous early ranchers and characters, Bill Keyes, the area has been heavily visited by hikers and rock climbers but as of yet nobody has offered a satisfying explanation for its construction. The most likely and reasonable justification for it is that it was where the man stored his explosives or perhaps even some of the bullion or bags of gold he wrenched from the ground. Bill Keyes was a miner along with being a rancher and also ran a mill for crushing gold ore that was utilized by scads of local miners, usually for a percentage or fee. Some have accused him of being a little less than honest in his transactions and that he might have been "high grading", a term for stealing the most valuable nuggets from a mine or mill, and that this was where he stashed his booty. But no proof has ever been offered and when it comes to gold, everyone believes the *other* guy has sticky fingers. I'm not sure the cave and its iron door can even be definitely traced to Keyes, so who knows *who* really built and used the thing.

Now there is another story about the door, and it is one I have heard more than a few times surrounding other such odd constructions all over the west, but it contains all the ingredients for a good mystery and I share it here. The tale goes that a local family had a horribly disfigured and mentally impaired son, huge and monstrous who they hid away from sight and society by locking him up in this rock and iron dungeon. The father would bring him food and sustenance but the poor creature spent his days and nights a virtual prisoner in this lonely cell.

Until one day when the father came to the place and found the door open and his deformed son gone!

In some versions of the story the son then goes on a Frankenstein-like rampage across the countryside, but in others he is never seen again and like all good monster stories told around a desert campfire "might still be out there waiting for an unwary traveler". I myself used the theme of this campfire myth as the seed for one of my western horror novellas entitled *The Charred Man* (available on Amazon) but as far as I know, nobody was ever kept in the Joshua Tree iron door cave. At least, I hope not! Being out in that searing heat locked in a cave would truly be a vision of hell.

Since we're down in the Joshua Tree area, I'll add one more oddity to this little chapter as it's always been a favorite of mine – The Barry Storm Jade Mine. Now technically, it lies at the very end of what's considered the Mojave proper and the beginning of the lower Colorado desert range, but for our purposes we'll include it here.

"Barry Storm", or John Griffith Climenson as he was born, was an eccentric author, miner and colorful desert character right out of an old movie. In fact, he was known to Hollywood, as one of his books *Thunder God's Gold* was made into a 1948 western drama starring Glen Ford and Ida Lupino titled *Lust for Gold* by Columbia Pictures and is still available if anyone is interested. It's actually pretty entertaining (though definitely a "B" picture) and also incorporates the idea of a high arch which points out the entrance to a mine when the full moon shines on it. Sound familiar? Just like the "Shaman's Eye" above.

But it's the later part of his life and its connection with Joshua Tree NP that interests me. Being a life-long fan of gold mining and lost mine stories and superstitions, Barry Storm claimed that one day while out in the desert down in the Pinto Basin area of what later became the park, he happened to see a trio of strange silver flying discs in the sky. Intrigued, he watched as they started to hover over a particular spot and then started shining beams of light down upon the slope of a small hill, causing the ground to emit a glow and sparkle. They then zoomed away and Storm felt compelled to go directly to the area and see what was being shown to him. Upon reaching the little hill, he started to dig and claimed that he found a string of ancient Mayan beads along with some other small artifacts, but then soon located a good deposit of jade and decided to stake a claim. He named the little venture the "Barry Storm Jade Mine" and then went on to claim that the ancient Mayans had mined there for the beautiful jade they fashioned into the intricate and fascinating funeral masks in which they buried their dead rulers and priests. How he deduced that I really have no clue, but for a guy who claimed that UFOs showed him where to dig, I guess the "logic" is inescapable. He spent the last decade of his life, from the early 1960's until his death in 1971 camped on the location, sometimes allowing visitors to try their luck in his little mine or twisting their ears with his tales of lost gold mines, flying saucers and questionable archaeological "facts" that he claimed backed up some of his more outrageous historical claims. Upon his death, the mine was abandoned and allowed to fall into disrepair.

The park service put a fence across the little road that led to his claim, but it can still be seen if you follow the Black Eagle Mine Road down about six or seven miles, and then look to your right near a small wash that crosses off to the south side of the road. If you park there, you can hike the roughly mile and a half along the faint road and come to the ruins and foundations of Barry Storm's mine. The shuttered shaft is still there, along with the ruins of his cabin, explosives storage room, burnt trailer and general junk and debris of a small desert mining operation. You can also still find chunks and pieces of the jade Storm was mining, but it is mainly of low or inferior grade and not particularly valuable. But it's the ambiance of the place that is its most rewarding and mysterious attribute. Standing on a spot where a man claimed to have been directed by aliens to dig, then actually found something, then spent years alone living out in that searing heat and arid dryness far from friends and family makes for a compelling visit. If you do venture down there, make sure you have plenty of water and a vehicle that can handle deep sand, because the park service has pulled many a stuck car (and sometimes bodies, like the poor Dutch couple found down there in 2011) out of the area because people didn't read the warning signs or heed the temperature alerts. It's not worth dying over.

Since this chapter is a rather eclectic compilation of oddities and mysteries without much rhyme or reason other than they fascinate me, I'm going to round it out by including some of the rather bizarre and shocking old news articles I have come across during my years of research and collecting. The Mojave has always been a source of excitement and adventure, and some of these happenings, though many years ago, shine a light on some classic horrors and skullduggery. Just remember they come from a time when political correctness was not exactly the forte of newspapers and reporters.

The first comes from the January 28th, 1910 edition of *The Los Angeles Herald* and concerns the morbid and murderous doings of the "Abo Pass Gang", a band of outlaws who had a rather unique way of getting their victims to talk.

BURNED FOOT POINTS TO CRIME

MOJAVE DESERT FIND VEILED IN MYSTERY WORK OF ABO PASS GANG IS SUGGESTED

Scorched Member Laced in High Top Boot an Indication of Band's Method of Forcing Victims to Reveal Treasure

[Special to The Herald.] SAN BERNARDINO, Jan. 27. The find of a human foot on the Mojave Desert, laced into a high top boot and bearing indications of having been burned, has caused widespread excitement among the miners and officials of the desert regions in the southwest. It is believed that the gruesome find points to a murder mystery, possibly the work of the Abo Pass robbers, who, for many months, have terrorized settlers along the Arizona-New Mexico border line. The evidence of the flesh of the foot having been burned strengthens the theory that the Abo Pass Gang has extended its operations to California. This band of robbers and murderers have used a peculiar method to force their victims to point out the hiding places of their money. If they refuse to tell where their treasure is located the robbers, who travel in a band of a dozen, bind and saturate the feet of their victims with oil, and in some cases their entire bodies. If they then refuse to tell they are burned alive. It is now said that the three men who were burned in this manner at Ash Fork were the victims of this gang. One of the men died in the Phoenix county hospital from injuries he received. At the Abo Pass, Mr. and Mrs. Espiasano were overpowered by a gang of armed men and when they refused to state where their wealth was hidden, they were covered with oil. They surrendered their hidden treasure when matches were struck to ignite the oil. Charles Ray was also a victim of the same gang, the robbers securing $250 in the same manner. It is said that the officers of New Mexico and Arizona will unite and appeal to both the federal governments of the United States and Mexico for assistance, it being believed that the operations of the gang extend in the latter country. The human foot was found by D. F. Watson within a few hundred yards of the Colorado river in a lonely gulch known on the desert as the Jamestown crossroad. It plainly had been burned and a portion of the upper part of the boot showed where the flames ate into the leather.

Sounds like a group of desperate men whose hands you'd rather not fall into! The Mojave was full of such characters and this next article, also from *The Los Angeles Herald*, November 14th, 1910 details another gang at work.

CORONER AND PARTY TO PROBE DESERT MYSTERY

SAN BERNARDINO, Nov. 13. - A desert tragedy that may develop into a sensational murder mystery has roused the county authorities into action, and under the direction of Coroner C. D. Van Wie a party of men led by Deputy Sheriff West of Needles is now headed across the Mojave waste for Ibex, where, according to the story of one Ike Middleton, an old desert prospector, a human body is lying partially covered by weeds and sand. Middleton's story is startling but agitating (sic) incomplete. He tells the Needles officers that he trailed a gang of robbers who rifled his cabin at Ibex across the desert sands to a small oasis a number of miles away and that as he neared the vegetation about the water hole he detected a strong odor. Frightened by the thought of what he believes had occurred, he made only a hasty investigation. The vegetation about the water had been brushed apart and some of it thrown over a rudely-constructed and half-covered grave, in which he says he believes he saw a form resembling a human. At the sight of the object he thinks is a murdered and half-buried man, he retreated, hastening with all speed to Needles. The officers place credence in Middleton's half-complete tale from the fact no cattle are herded in the Ibex country and that there has never been a disposition on the part of miners and prospectors to bury dead animals, either cattle, coyotes or horses. It is a week's trip to the water hole and back to Needles, and word is not expected from the officers before the expiration of that time.

I never found a follow-up report to this article so I don't know what the officers found when they returned from their week's trip to the water hole in question. I like how the authorities decided to "place credence" in the old prospector's tale as no one out in those parts ever bothered burying their dead animals! Classic.

Now this next one actually claims a murder mystery solved, but not the one just offered. It involves the same coroner and general location in the Mojave, even happening later in the same year, but as far as I can tell is not the same case.

LOS ANGELES HERALD, MARCH 19th, 1910

DESERT MYSTERY IS SOLVED BY SKELETON

EDWARD CLIFFORD DIES ON THE MOJAVE WASTE

Pack of Miner Establishes Identity of Person Who Left Needles Last Summer and Not Since Heard From

SAN BERNARDINO, March 18. - A human skeleton found in the salt beds sixty miles west of Calzona, this county, solves the mystery and tragic disappearance of Edward Clifford, a well-known desert miner, who left Needles early last summer, never to be seen again. Coroner Van Wie was today notified by Justice Harper of Calzona of the discovery of the skeleton believed to be that of Clifford. The finding of the pack, portions of clothing and dually the human bones mutely tells the terrible tale of the end of another of the countless victims of the arid waste. In the pack and clothing, which Clifford had evidently shed in his terrible delirium, were found letters, money and various other articles which identify Clifford. The skeleton and pack were found by Andreas Heyman and Robert Martin.

Whoa! The area around Needles, California was quite the dangerous and perilous place back in 1910, huh? I like how the article states that the bones "mutely tells the terrible tale of the end of another of the countless victims of the arid waste." The Mojave can be beautiful and transcendent, but to those who find themselves lost or without water it really can be an arid waste and ultimately, a graveyard.

Want another one? Okay, I saved this last article as it's a classic for both its sensationalism and complete lack of tact. Again, remember this was from a time when physical impairments were often associated with intelligence and moral properties. It also comes from *The Los Angeles Herald*, but in this case a bit earlier, from the June 11th, 1904 edition:

PARTNER OF SLAIN PROSPECTOR SWEARS HE'LL TRACK SUSPECTED HUNCHBACK TILL HE'S AVENGED

W. G. Carpenter Borrows a Revolver and Starts for Bakersfield to Take Up Trail

BURNING with wrath and determined to avenge the murder of his former comrade in business, Carpenter, a local mining man, left Los Angeles Thursday night for Piute mountain, he goes, in an effort to trail down the slayer of J. A. Valentine and bring him to account for his foul crime. Before leaving this city Carpenter carefully armed himself for the journey. He carried with him a brace of revolvers and plenty of ammunition, swearing as he boarded the train that he would run the murderer down if he has to traverse the ends of the earth. While the evidence is very meager, Carpenter believes that Alexander Pontan, the hunchback who has been under suspicion, is guilty of Valentine's murder. From the few circumstances at hand it appears to him that the victim of the brutal crime was lured to his death by Pontan, and Carpenter is determined to follow the misshapen suspect if need be to the borders of Mexico. It is believed that the murderer lured his victim to an old cabin on the wild, lonely mountainside, under the pretense of having mining claims there which he wanted examined. Before Valentine's body was discovered it had partially decomposed and the murderer was probably many days' journey away. So Carpenter may be gone many months before he returns to Los Angeles with the murder of his partner and friend avenged. The chase will be carried on in a rough, wild country and will be untiring and relentless. Well-armed before he left Los Angeles, Carpenter borrowed a revolver from H. Tostman of the El Monte saloon on Main street, for whom Valentine went to examine the alleged mining claim of Pontan's.

"Valentine had my revolver with him when he was killed," said Carpenter, by way of excuse. "I would rather have that one because I am used to it, but there will probably be red tape to go through before I can get it and there is no time to be lost. It is too bad that Valentine had no chance to use the gun, but he was a man who was so good himself that he suspected no one and his having a gun with him was only a matter of form. This Pontan was a fearful creature, who lived on liquor and 'dope,' and I figure that he never did have any mining claims and from the looks of things I suspect he shot my partner on the first night they landed in the little cabin and then took the team and wagon they had hired at Mojave for the trip and started for the nearest saloon to spend the money. I'm certainly set on finding that man and meeting him face to face. I've got a number of personal questions which I want to put to him and incidentally any of his friends who can get word to him had better advise him to change his ways of living right now while he has a chance."

Carpenter is a man of about 40, who looks fully capable of following any trail upon which he sets out. That he will bring the murderer of his friend back dead or alive is firmly believed by those who know him.

(Special to The Herald.) BAKERSFIELD, June 10—New developments are coming to light in the Valentine murder case and Sheriff Kelly is making every effort, with the meager facts in his possession, to ferret out the perpetrator of the atrocious crime. He has notified the officers at all points on the desert as far as Inyo county to be on the lookout for the hunchback, Pontan, and it would seem, in case the latter H alive (sic), that it would be impossible for him to get through the country unobserved. Word was received from Mojave this morning that W. G. Carpenter of Los Angeles, a friend of Valentine, is at that place and in conjunction with Deputy Sheriff Dearborn they have found that the trap with which Valentine and Pontan went to the mine was secured from Lohman & Perris, liverymen of that place, and that it was on June 4 by a third party, who exhibited a considerable amount of money and claimed he had sold a mining claim out in the Kelso canyon. He also told this story to the ticket agent at the depot, where he bought a ticket for the north. His destination was not learned. The man is described as being a heavily built fellow, dark mustache and complexion, about five feet seven inches tall. He talked with a German accent.

Pontan at Large

No trace of Pontan has as yet been discovered and it may be possible that he also was a victim and that this third man was the murderer of both. As soon as possible Sheriff Kelly will make a careful examination of the trail from the cabin through Jawbone canyon as far as the eighteen-mile house to see if there is any evidence of a murder having been committed along the road, as it is believed that if the theory that Pontan was killed should prove true his grave will be found along the road between these points. A year ago Alexander Pontan and Ike Bryson, son of millionaire John Bryson of Los Angeles, made a trip to the same mining claim visited with fatal insults by Valentine. On that trip, according to Bryson, Pontan played the part of maniac, compelling Bryson at the point of a gun to make a wild drive of several hours through the rugged mountain region. Finally, the horses ran away, the rig was smashed and in the general mix-up Bryson escaped. This would tend to bear out the theory that Pontan was the murderer, but again the question arises from the evidence secured at Mojave, what has become of Pontan and who is the third party who returned the team to the livery stable? This man, whoever he is, now has six days' start of the officers, and on account of the slight description of him he stands a good chance of making his escape unless Carpenter, the avenger, succeeds in bringing him to bay.

Now THAT is an article! Yes, the description of the suspect, Alexander Pontan, as a "hunchback and fearful creature, who lived on liquor and "dope" is way over the top and certainly inflammatory, but man, what a story! And it continues – this from *The Los Angeles Herald*, March 10th, 1904:

MINER ON HUNT FOR MURDERER

Valentine's Friend Will Investigate Death

If J. A. Valentine, the Los Angeles miner who was found murdered in a lone cabin on Piute mountain, ever prayed as did Kipling's soldier that "God send us a trusty chum," his prayer was answered and because he has for months had for a bunk mate (?) W. G. Carpenter, and the dead man's body will find friends and relatives to care for it and his murder will in all probability be avenged. The details of the crime are meager but the information gathered from different sources by Valentine's friends outline the story of a murder unusual in its cunning and depravity. Valentine was found dead in a cabin on Piute mountain. There were four bullet holes in his head and in his left hand he clutched a 38-caliber Colt's revolver. His papers were scattered about the cabin floor and all money and jewels were gone from his person. Alexander Pontan, the man who is thought to have induced him to make his trip and who alone accompanied him, was nowhere to be found. W. G. Carpenter, comrade in mining ventures with Valentine since the beginning of this year and his roommate at the St. Elmo (sic), left last night for the scene of the murder, well-armed and determined to avenge his partner's death if possible.

His first work will be to find the relatives of Valentine and make some final disposition of the body and then he will follow relentlessly the man who did the murder and leave no stone unturned to bring him to justice.

No Mercy for him

"The evidence of this crime is heavy against Pontan," said Carpenter last night. "His record shows him a bad man and any person who could conceive and carry out such an atrocious murder at this one deserves absolutely no mercy."

Pontan was a cook by profession and worked with mining outfits and ranches. He was a hunchback, 55 years old and a little over five feet in height. He had black heavy eyebrows, large protruding eyes and a black mustache, his frame was large but his legs were crooked, which made him walk with a limp.

According to the reports of those who have had dealings with him he was as misshapen in soul as body. He was a drug and liquor fiend of the worst kind. He is known over all the Southern California mining district as a "bad man," of the sort that boasts of being one. Col. J. N. Ashby, president of the Papago Mining company, hired Pontan last year as a cook at his camp. He says that the man had finally to be discharged because no one felt safe with him in camp. Before leaving Pontan discharged three shots from his revolver, which came dangerously near Col. Ashby's head but which he excused as being accidentally fired. This man came into Los Angeles about two weeks ago and was employed for a time by H. Tostmann at the El Monte saloon on North Main street. He told Tostmann that while out cooking for a mining camp he had come across a valuable claim and pleaded with his employer that he investigate it and offered him the greater part of the claim if he would furnish the funds to open the mine. Tostmann finally agreed to send Valentine out to the alleged claim to look it over and for this purpose Valentine left with the hunchback a week ago last Wednesday night. Valentine carried with him about $300 for expense money. The two went from here to Mojave, where they hired a livery rig and drove into the mountains. There Valentine, alone with this man of dreadful shape and unsavory reputation, took up his camp in an empty hunters' cabin.

Body Is Found

No one knows anything of the story from that point until someone found his decomposed body with the four gaping wounds in the head. For the rest the investigation to be made by Carpenter must be awaited. The following letter was received here yesterday morning by H. Yarnell, owner of several claims on the Piute mountain, from Mrs. E. B. Kersey, the postmistress at Piute, and outside of the press dispatches this is the only news received of the murder in Los Angeles: There was a brutal murder committed here at the old Esperanza cabin and the coroner buried the man yesterday morning. From three letters found in the cabin the man is supposed to be J. A. Valentine. Alex Pontan is believed to be the murderer. Valentine was shot through the top of the head. He was found Saturday, June 4. It is supposed he was killed about the first. Alex Pontan and another man hired a livery rig at Mojave and were seen to stop at the sixteen-mile house at 10 a.m. Please do all you can to have Pontan arrested If he returns to Los Angeles. If Ike Bryson had done what he should have done when Pontan held him up last August, this would not have happened. Please let us know as soon as he is arrested. He is no man to be left loose. The reference to Bryson in the letter is of a time when Pontan worked for a miner of that name who said Pontan several times threatened his life. Valentine was a Mason and a popular man wherever he went. He was well known all over the west in mining circles. He and Carpenter

156

were to have started for Mexico in July on a large mining contract which they had made there.

I'd love to know how this most excellent murder mystery played out, but unfortunately I have not been able to uncover any more information. The culprits and victims have all faded back into the mists of time. I guess it's just like so many mysteries one encounters out in the great Mojave; something that leaves you scratching your head and wondering just what the devil was going on?

Finis

I hope you've enjoyed this first volume of Mojave Mysteries, as I said earlier, it's more my personal cabinet of curiosities I love to entertain myself and others with, rather than an exhaustive study of any one subject. I find the desert to be such a wondrous place, simultaneously filled with both danger and romance in equal proportions and always ready to confound or perplex. If you visit the great Mojave, and I sincerely hope you get the chance, please remember to bring enough water and supplies, as like the ocean in the old saying; the minute you don't respect it, it will kill you. But I can readily assure you that the reward for your efforts will be paid back thrice fold in amazing natural beauty, spiritual refreshment and of course, enough bizarre and captivating mysteries to last a lifetime.

See you next time!

We hope you enjoyed author M.L. Behrman's "Mojave Mysteries, Vol. 1" and want to thank you for your purchase. We invite you check out his Western Thriller series featuring everyone's favorite monster hunting cowboy J. Everett Earl. All available from Amazon.Com.

Current releases in the series:

The Wyoming Howler – A mysterious man-like animal is prowling the range in a remote area of Wyoming, killing men and cattle alike. Cowboy and hunter J. Everett Earl is hired to track the beast down and kill it before he becomes its next victim!

The Charred Man – A hideously deformed and disfigured fiend haunts the hills around Bisbee, Arizona in the 1880's kidnapping and killing without mercy. Can cowboy J. Everett Earl find the killer and put an end to his reign of terror?

The Canyon Devil – High in the mountains surrounding Death Valley, a creature from the mists of time preys on the poor miners and prospectors of the area, its snapping jaws and dripping teeth leaving few clues as to its identity. There's only one man for this job!

Ghost Tribe - The Curse of Custer's Gold - A lost treasure, Indian renegades and a "tribe" of strange blood-thirsty creatures lie in wait for J. Everett Earl as he guides a private expedition into the heart of the sacred Black Hills in search of General Custer's secret gold hoard!

Join us on online at:

www.facebook.com/mojavemysteries

www.mlbehrman.com

www.youtube.com/mojavemysteries

www.twitter.com/mojavemysteries

ISBN-10:1540583864
ISBN-13:978-1540583864
Copyright 2016
M.L. Behrman
All Rights Reserved. V.M. LLC

Made in the USA
Las Vegas, NV
09 July 2021

26196991R00089